Pitman
Education
Library

An Induction Course
for teaching in further education and industry

An Induction Course
for teaching in further education and industry

PATRICIA MacMILLAN & LEN POWELL

 PITMAN PUBLISHING

First published 1973

Sir Isaac Pitman and Sons Ltd
Pitman House, Parker Street, Kingsway, London WC2B 5PB
PO Box 46038, Portal Street, Nairobi, Kenya

Sir Isaac Pitman (Aust.) Pty Ltd
Pitman House, 158 Bouverie Street, Carlton, Victoria 3053, Australia

Pitman Publishing Corporation
6 East 43rd Street, New York NY 10017, USA

Sir Isaac Pitman (Canada) Ltd
495 Wellington Street West, Toronto 135, Canada

The Copp Clark Publishing Company
517 Wellington Street West, Toronto 135, Canada

Cased edition: ISBN 0 273 00184 1
Paperback edition: ISBN 0 273 00185 X

Text set in 11/13 IBM Baskerville, printed by photolithography,
and bound in Great Britain at The Pitman Press, Bath
G4690/4691 : 15

Introduction

what about learning

This is a book about teaching: it is based on the notion that teaching is an art of communication. But like all other arts, such as music or painting, poetry or pottery, it requires more than just a basic talent, it requires the discipline of rules and theory, a framework of reference within which it can be directed towards objectives that withstand philosophical testing.

Teaching, then, is communicating, and this includes doing and acting in the practical setting of the classroom. It is, however, more than transmitting information, more than exchanging ideas, it is the active dynamic expression of responsible involvement in the total educative process. If we believe that education begins at birth and continues throughout life, then we see it as a constantly changing process which involves each one of us in learning and teaching. But when we set out purposefully to educate others, it indicates that we not only share a common concern for future generations, but also that we, to some degree, are willing to accept both the responsibility and public accountability which the teacher's role naturally and inexorably presupposes. Insofar as training is part of education, those of us who train others in industrial skills have a similar, if somewhat less evident responsibility . . . we too should share in this concern.

Because teaching is more than acting and doing in a classroom, because what we do as teachers today will be reflected in future society, teaching must essentially involve us in constant analysis and constructive critical thinking about what we are doing.

It is therefore the responsibility of every teacher and every training officer to study the theory of his professionalism and to try to understand the nature of his role in relation to his students and society. This clearly calls for reading and further study. But since the individual who is about to begin teaching or training is primarily preoccupied with thinking about his own performance as a communicator and motivator, this induction course centres on these practical issues. In that principles and theories contribute to the precision with which teachers make tactical decisions, these are included but only in sufficient detail to support the practical work. The objective is to enable a new teacher to perform with confidence so that he is freed from the constraints of apprehension and indecision and is thus able to engage in more serious intellectual consideration of education.

The book is designed for a four-stage course with precise and limited behavioural objectives. It is supported by film and transparencies and constitutes the 'handout' for a course under the guidance of a group tutor.

In brief, the course has the following form:

OBJECTIVE

To enable new teachers, instructors and training officers to communicate confidently and effectively and to experience the role of the teacher in four dissimilar learning arrangements.

SUB-OBJECTIVES

At the end of the first week

To lead a fifteen minute discussion following a set pattern and with a stated objective.

At the end of the second week

To lecture, following a set pattern and with a stated objective. During the talk, to use a chalkboard, flip-chart or similar writing surface.

At the end of the third week

To give a lesson with stated behavioural objectives. During the lesson to use an overhead projector giving reasons for using it and to demonstrate with materials and equipment. To prepare and use a brief objective test to assess the effectiveness of the lesson.

At the end of the fourth week

To complete a learning package with stated behavioural objectives and with a pre-test and a post-test. The package to include
the script of a loop film, a tape-slide presentation, a video-taped
presentation or a tape-text presentation.

The course aims at enabling the new teacher to perform these
four roles: discussion manager, lecturer, teacher and resource
manager, at a high level of competency so as to give him a
personal standard of excellence of which he knows he is capable.
Once he has experienced these roles he will be better fitted to
practice them and to analyse and understand method theory and
thence the professional studies of his occupation.

This book has been prompted by that very important docu-
ment, the James Report . . . (Teacher Education and Training . . .
a Report by a Committee of Inquiry appointed by the Secretary
of State for Education and Science under the Chairmanship of
Lord James of Rusholme).

The report recommends very urgent immediate review of
teacher training at all levels. In Chap. 2 para. 27, James points
out that many teachers for Further Education are recruited from
other occupations 'and bring their accumulated experience of
industry, commerce and the public service to their work in
further education. In most cases, it would be unreasonable to
expect them to undertake full-time courses of pre-service training . . . (sic) . . . They might be required to take, during the first
two years of service, training courses amounting to not less than
three months full-time or the equivalent, and wherever possible
such courses should include an induction period of not less than
three or four weeks full time.'

We believe that the adequate preparation of the professional
person coming into Further Education teaching is an increasingly
urgent matter. A man may be a first rate lawyer or plumber or
butcher or personnel manager or banker or candle-stick maker,
but we know that does not automatically make him a first rate
teacher or communicator. Furthermore he is often unaware of
the new technological innovations which have been developed
for the teaching profession. Most of us new to teaching rely on

our own experiences to direct us when we face a class of students for the first time.

It is very much a hit-or-miss affair and it often totally disregards the general level of audio-visual communications in the outside world to which the young student has become accustomed. An induction course should orientate the professional to the total teaching-learning process. It should rule out the hit-and-miss characteristic of the untrained teacher and clearly demonstrate how best he can communicate his skills and knowledge in the classroom. This book aims at no more and no less than that.

ACKNOWLEDGMENTS

This course has been developed over a period of years and has involved a great deal of testing, modifying and validating. We are very grateful to those organizations in industry and the hospital service where we have practised, and in particular to the General Training Department of BOAC.

Bill Stephen and Bernard Lovell of Garnett College read the manuscript and we appreciate their generous and excellent advice.

Judith Cole made the drawings and Doreen Heatley typed the manuscript.

Course Plan

OBJECTIVES

1. To prepare and lead a discussion.
2. To prepare and give a talk.
3. To prepare and teach a lesson.
4. To prepare and test a learning package.

The course combines training in performance competencies with the relevant theoretical studies drawn from philosophy, sociology, psychology and management theory.

MODULE I

TALKING WITH STUDENTS AND OTHER MATTERS

Unit 1	Study Session	Communication
	Micro-training	Non-verbal signals
	Exercise	One-way two-way communication
	Films	One-way two-way communication
Unit 2	Study Session	Behavioural objectives
	Exercise	Writing behavioural objectives
	Micro-training	Closing a talk
	Exercise	Closing a talk
Unit 3	Study Session	Testing and assessing
	Exercise	Preparing an objective test (for Unit 8)
		Preparing a verbalized rating scale (for Unit 5)
	Micro-training	Establishing Rapport
	Film	Rapport

AN INDUCTION COURSE

Unit 4	Study Session	Managing a discussion
	Exercise	Preparation of a discussion
	Micro-training	Opening a discussion
	Film	Managing a discussion

Unit 5	Practical exercise	LEADING A DISCUSSION

MODULE II

TALKING TO STUDENTS AND OTHER MATTERS

Unit 6	Study Session	Factors which influence learning 1. Perception
	Micro-training	Opening a talk
	Study Session	Factors which influence learning 2. Behavioural patterns of adolescence
	Micro-training	Extended opening of a talk
	Study Session	Factors which influence learning 3. Theories of learning
	Practical exercise	Learning exercises
	Micro-training	Use of chalkboard and flip-chart

Unit 7	Exercise	Preparation of a talk (a) objective (b) test (c) notes

Unit 8	Practical exercise	GIVING A TALK

MODULE III

TEACHING STUDENTS

Unit 9	Study Session	The analysis of a lesson
	Micro-training	Closing a lesson
	Film	Closing a lesson

2

Module I

Talking with students

and other matters

Introduction to Module I

Teaching is the art of causing learning

A newly hired travelling salesman wrote his first sales report to the home office. It stunned the brass in the sales department because it was obvious the new 'hope' was an illiterate, for he wrote:

> 'I have seen this outfit which they ain' never bought a dimes worth of nothing from us and I sole them a couple hundred tousand dollars of guds. I am now going to Chicawgo.'

Before the illiterate could be given the heave-to by the sales manager along came this letter from Chicago:

> 'I cum hear and sole them haff a millyon.'

Fearful if he did, and fearful if he didn't fire the man, the sales manager dumped the problem in the lap of the president.

The following morning the ivory tower members were amazed to see the two letters posted on the bulletin board — and this memo from the president tacked above:

> 'We ben spending two much time trying to spel instead of trying to sel. Let's wach thoes sails. I want everybody should read these letters from Booch, who is on the rode doin a grate job for us, and you should go out and do like he done.'
>
> *from a Canadian magazine.*

MORAL: A good idea in the student is worth two in the teacher.

Unit I

Study Session

Communication

MOTIVATION TO WORK

Whatever else he may hope to do, the teacher spends most of his working life deliberately communicating with other people, and a great deal of this is deliberately structured to make them work. At the onset it would be well to ask what it is that makes people want to work: indeed, since the teacher is to some greater degree than other people, involved in others' lives, it would also be well to ask what it is that gives them happiness or satisfaction through work and through life.

In his book *Authority and the Individual,*[1] Bertrand Russell wrote the following:

> 'If human life is not to become dusty and uninteresting it is important to realize that there are things that have a value which is independent of utility. Monotony may be more deadening than an alternation of delight and agony . . . to most people not only spontaneity but some kind of personal pride is necessary for happiness.'

Although a great deal has been written about the reasons why students want to learn, the most valuable information about motivation at this level comes from studies of people at work.

Professor Frederick Herzberg[2] and his colleagues concluded that certain features of work which gave rise to a sense of achievement, recognition and responsibility, and indeed the content of work itself were of prime importance in motivating people to work.

Professor Fred Emery,[3] in research work carried out in Norway, concluded that for motivation to work, six psychological needs should, ideally be met. They are:

(i) the need for the content of the job to be reasonably demanding of the worker in terms of other than sheer endurance, and yet provide variety (not necessarily novelty);

(ii) the need to be able to learn on the job and to go on learning;

(iii) the need to make decisions that the individual can call his own;

(iv) the need for some minimal degree of social support and recognition in the workplace;

(v) the need to be able to relate what he does and produces to his social life;

(vi) the need to feel that the job leads to some sort of desirable future (Fig. 1).

So there are motivational pressures that make us willing and ready to work and all of them are created and sustained in some way or another by communication with other people. And what is more, the manner and mode of these communication processes can enhance or destroy all the physical provision, all the earlier hopes, all the determination that have been gathered in to sustain the effort during trial. So we ought now to consider what communication is about.

NON-VERBAL COMMUNICATION

We communicate with other people for a variety of reasons. In our view the following are important — to give information, to get information, to express our feelings, to arouse feelings and to think things out. Each of these is intended to effect some change in the behaviour of somebody else and to do this we may use gestures, sounds, pictures, words, symbols or even smells. It is relevant, therefore, to enquire of any communication, 'What will it *do* to him?'. The critical consequence is the changed behaviour to which it gives rise. Equally, but not so evidently, the communicator may be changed as a result of communicating so that it is also relevant to ask, 'What is this doing to me?' Is it, for example, giving personal gratification, soothing a sense of guilt or recognizing the listener as a responsible person?

Communication, then, aims at behaviour change.

Fig. 1 Motivation to work

The most primitive and often the most powerful communication takes place non-verbally. Some signs have been designed to take the place of words in giving information. They are called paralinguistic symbols and include road signs, danger signals and so on. These are part of the language of civilized living and ignorance of this language invokes a range of responses from admiration at one end of the scale to distrust at the other. Take, for example, a punched card wages slip, this may evoke the reaction: 'clever' or 'I don't trust computers'.

Signs made by people — protolinguistic signs — are of fundamental importance to teachers (Fig. 2). They include movements, demeanour, smiles, gestures, winks and wrinkles. These may be made unconsciously or they may be beyond our control, like blushing or the dropping of the eyelids, or they may be made consciously and controlled, like gestures. At college there is a strange tendency for students to need and seek meaning from a teacher's protolinguistic behaviour: on the other hand new teachers often expect to receive accurate verbal information and to regard protolinguistic signs as unimportant. The

Fig. 2 Non-verbal signs

students very often *want* to receive information face to face:
teachers, too often, prefer it in writing.

MANNERISMS

Nervousness on the part of the teacher may be linked with
insincerity and lack of knowledge, and in ordinary social inter-
course this linkage is often valid. A student finds it difficult to
believe that his teacher could possibly be nervous simply because
he has to talk to students. This is an important and highly consequential fact. Many people are nervous when called upon to talk
to a group: the fear derives from the disparity in numbers, from
our intuitive knowledge of group behaviour, from our desire to
be as superior in the role of speaker as we are in the social hierarchy and from our unwillingness to be assessed by *how* we
communicate.

   This initial nervousness gives rise to certain unconscious avoidance tactics. The new teacher, conscious of the quizzical gaze of
twenty pairs of eyes, feels uncommonly exposed. So he looks,
not at his students but at the cool, kindly, unreactive top corner
of the back of the room . . . and feels easier for it. Each time his
gaze drops, they are there — twenty pairs of eyes, and he looks
back at the wall; so inevitably, the conditioning process continues until, without really knowing it, he invariably talks into
space. He could, of course, contemplate the chalkboard for
spiritual massage, or the view through the window. But the
result is the same. He behaves as though he dislikes the very
sight of students and they, for their part, reciprocate this implied
attitude.

   There are other avoidance tactics — nervous walking, reading
notes even when they are not there, observing fingers or juggling
with chalk. None seems reprehensible, all become established
during the first critical weeks, all set up unnecessary social
barriers which students resent.

   Indeed, we would do well to train ourselves to display non-
verbal signals that fit in with everyday social behaviour. When
we begin a lesson, and whatever we say, our body should signal
a greeting, 'Hello, I'm delighted to see each one of you'. At the
end, it should say, 'Well, that's all for now and it's been pleasant.

Goodbye'. More than any other part of our signalling system, our eyes give these messages, helped along by our hands, head, feet, sighs, grunts, and — if we use after-shave — our smell. This is not to say that mannerisms are bad, in fact, any mannerism which we normally display at home or at parties is likely to be a kind of trade-mark of our personality — something rather like-able — but the ones we establish through apprehension when we begin teaching are impediments to the learning process. Non-verbal communication, then, is an important component of communication.

Paralinguistic signs should be divested of mystery or ambiguity (we should be able to distinguish between the lady and gentle-men on toilet doors) and protolinguistic language should be understood and controlled by those who are in authority. As a rule, this calls for some training and some experience.

Micro-training Exercise
Controlling non-verbal signals

Each group member, in turn, to stand in front of the group and introduce himself to them, stating his name, where he lives and the college in which he will teach. As he does so, he should look at each group member and try to imply by his demeanour that he is introducing himself, and that he is pleased to meet group members. As he speaks he should try to think about each member as an individual human being and not about the con-struction of what he is saying. He should avoid thinking that he is talking to 'a group' and focus on talking to this person, and this person and so on.

The process is helped if members have easily-seen name plates in front of them and in appropriate circumstances use first as well as surnames.

This exercise is more valuable if closed circuit television is used. If the speaker is recorded on video-tape the shot should be in big close-up. It should be played back *immediately* and com-mented on for non-verbal signs only. Each presentation should occupy no more than 10 seconds with the opportunity for repeats if they are likely to be helpful. Playback without sound can emphasize the quality of the non-verbal components.

SPOKEN COMMUNICATION

If spoken communication is to stand a chance of being understood, the student must make six kinds of response to it. He must:

(i) *listen.* He may not understand the words but this response will give him foundation information. He will hear how loud the message sounds, whether it is said in anger, where the speaker is standing, whether it is rythmical and so on.

(ii) *compare.* He will compare the sounds he hears with those he has heard before and remembered. This is an active mental reaching-out-for-meaning process.

(iii) *recognize.* Here, he holds a group of sounds in his mind and recognizes them as a phrase or a sentence. The sequence may be meaningless but it will have an intonational pattern. The sequence —
  'clump crandulates turnfully'
fits into such a pattern whereas —
  'clump crand tun' does not.

(iv) *interpret.* Here the sequence provides components with meaning; words alone are frequently ambiguous and depend upon their context for meaning. Thus we can interpret,
  'Little children ape their parents'
whilst we cannot interpret,
  'Little purples ape their thoughts'.

(v) *comprehend.* Here we find the implication of the communication in terms of what we know about the situation in which it occurs. Thus, for example, 'I am working as hard as I can' may mean 'I want you to help me'; or 'You are early' may mean 'You are late'.

(vi) *believe.* Thus, for example, if a student said,
  'I saw a rattlesnake in the canteen',
he would be believed only in some parts of the world.

Equally, a teacher who says,
> 'This machine "remembers" the instructions you feed
> into it',

would be believed only by some students.
So there are six components:

1. listen   4. interpret
2. compare   5. comprehend
3. recognize   6. believe

Teaching is the art of causing these responses to happen and together they constitute the process of perception.

LEVELS OF COMMUNICATION

Perception is an active response to communication: it involves reaching for meaning and, to a greater or lesser degree, creating meaning. In all circumstances, the mode of communication which appears to lead most easily to successful understanding will be preferred to other modes since we are motivated by experiences which appear directed towards success and discouraged by those which seem to be directed towards failure. And since there is a link between intelligence and the efficiency of psychological reactions to sensory impressions, preferred modes of communication will, broadly speaking, vary with intelligence.

Roughly speaking less intelligent students need concrete evidence, particular examples and things to handle; average students rely heavily on visual information whilst highly intelligent ones cope happily with abstractions, generalizations, technical terms and mathematical relationships. Whatever our intelligence we tend to perceive what we expect to perceive, what we want to perceive and, at times, what we decide to perceive, or what we are told to perceive. Perception depends too, on age, ability, attitude, environment, social pressures, previous learning and so on and accuracy in perception is clearly enhanced by multi-channel communication — by seeing and smelling: seeing and hearing: hearing and touching for example.

LISTENING

So, efficient verbal communication is bedevilled with the effects of non-verbal signs and by the wayward character of perception. It is useful to look at one more aspect of the problem before seeking remedies. There are two reasons why we should never give information when somebody else is talking. First of all, speaking and listening simultaneously is difficult, just as it is difficult to understand two simultaneous conversations, and secondly we need to hear the sound of our own voice in order to check the accuracy of what we are saying.

Assuming we are talking to a student, the sequence of thinking that ensues is as follows: first, the student makes a guess about the meaning of what we are saying and generates an internal matching signal. If matching does not work, it is used as the basis for a neat guess and so on until a satisfactory match is obtained. Now notice that the listener's response is not an automatically translated version of what he hears, it is a programme of seeking and checking which leads up to the matching. And if he receives other, conflicting signals at the same time this process becomes difficult.

Looking at this more closely, the first guess probably derives, in part, from signposts in the form of intonations, inflexions, expressions and so on and in part, from a general knowledge of the semantic and contextual situation. Words, like the notes in music, are not enough to trigger understanding.

READING ABILITY

The problem of coping with words becomes most acute in reading since the information is unsupported by intonation or non-verbal signs. The difficulty people have in reading is evidenced by the fact that 31 per cent of the households in this country have twenty books or less[4] — and here the word 'book' refers to format and not content.

In one college of further education it was found that about a quarter of the white students had reading ages of between 9 and 11 years and there is no reason to believe that this college is in any way special. What is important is that most books in colleges of further education libraries and most textbooks used by the students have a readability suitable for reading ages of 17 years and upwards. Popular newspapers by comparison are pitched at reading ages of 13—14 years.[5]

It is therefore evident that one reason why many students avoid the library and do not read textbooks is simply because they are unable to do so with any degree of ease or success — they simply serve to remind the student of his inadequacy.

The most direct visual counterpart of non-verbal signals is the cartoon strip in which non-verbal messages are visually emphasized. This accounts for the attraction of this mode of communication to backward readers.

The scale and conversion table given in Fig. 3 is a pretty reliable means of measuring the readability of books and journals. Obviously it is unsuitable for certain material — poems, prayers and so on — but it is useful in persuading teachers to discover the problems that some — indeed many — students have in merely coming to terms with words. It is salutary to use it to assess the readability of, what may have been regarded as, a simple handout.

Fig. 3. GRAPH FOR ESTIMATING READABILITY

by Edward Fry, Rutgers University Reading Center, New Jersey

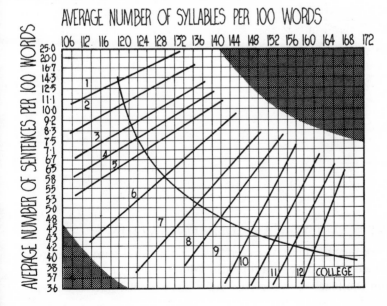

AVERAGE NUMBER OF SYLLABLES PER 100 WORDS

AVERAGE NUMBER OF SENTENCES PER 100 WORDS

AN INDUCTION COURSE

Directions   Randomly select 3 one hundred word passages from a book or an article. Plot average number of syllables and average number of words per sentence on graph to determine the grade level of the material. Choose more passages per book if great variability is observed and conclude that the book has uneven readability. Few books will fall in grey area but when they do grade level scores are invalid.

Example

	Syllables	Sentences
1st Hundred Words	124	6.6
2nd Hundred Words	141	5.5
3rd Hundred Words	158	6.8
AVERAGE	141	6.3

Readability 7th Grade

U.S. GRADE/UK READING AGE   APPROXIMATIONS

grade		reading age
1		6—7
2		7—8
3		8—9
4		9—10
5		10—11
6		11—12
7		12—13
8		13—14
9		14—15
10		15—16
11		16—17
12		17—18

ONE-WAY TWO-WAY COMMUNICATION

In the face of these observed facts, we would be unwise to rely exclusively upon communication that travels one way only — from the teacher to the student. What we must have is a means of monitoring and refining the student's interpretations, if possible, as they are made. With highly motivated mature students, this is less critical and may be achieved by recommending books and articles which support the information. Within the average classroom, however, it must come from face-to-face discussion, questioning and answering. And because intention is involved as well as content, the information must be provided genuinely to help the students to learn effectively: it must recognize that they matter, that they are responsible and that they want to learn.

Exercise

The objective of this exercise is to provide first-hand experience of the major distinction between one-way and two-way communication.

In the diagram (Fig. 4), the rectangles touch one another at corners or at mid-side points: each is twice as long as it is wide and all the angles between the lines are either 45° or 90°.

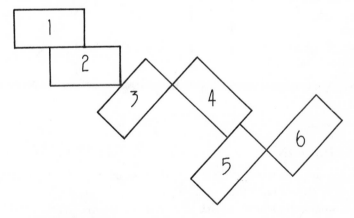

Fig. 4 Feed-back exercise 1
   [This exercise is reproduced from Leavitt: *Managerial Psychology*, 1964, by kind permission of the University of Chicago Press]

Each group member except the one chosen to instruct, has a blank sheet of paper on which he will draw the rectangles as they are described. The 'instructor' will stand with his back to the group who will remain completely silent during the exercise.

Using the diagram and in a businesslike manner, he will tell the group how to draw it and they will follow his instructions. He will use only verbal information.

The same instructor will now use two-way communication to teach his group to draw the diagram in Fig. 5. He will look at the group and encourage them to ask questions if they are unsure about a step. They can stop him when they wish to ask for clarification. He will use only verbal information. The learners must make every endeavour to get their drawings right.

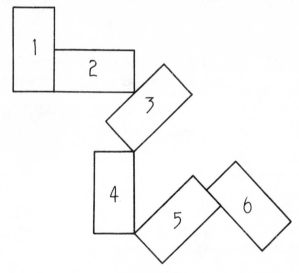

Fig. 5 Feed-back exercise 2

DISCUSSION

Discuss the emotions and effects of these examples of one-way and two-way communication.

Compare the findings with the generalizations given in the following notes 1 and 2.

NOTES

1. Communication may be one-way or two-way. One-way is faster, it protects the sender from recognizing his faults, it can be unreliable, it makes the receiver feel uneasy. If it is going to

be as efficient as it can be it must be planned and it must carry redundant information. It is useful in emergencies.

2. Two-way communication is slower, more accurate, noisy, often makes the sender feel he is being attacked but the receivers feel more sure of themselves.

3.

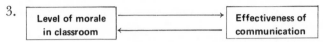

In all, falling morale is associated with rigidity, and conformity whilst rising morale derives from responsible human relationships.

As we communicate we can adopt one of three attitudes which reflect our intentions:

(i) Authoritative communication aiming at simplicity, order and personal gratification, which leads to restrictions, hostility and decreased feedback.

(ii) Persuasive communication which stems from established close relationships and sensitivity to human needs and emotions and so often aims at manipulation.

(iii) Collaborative communication which recognizes the student as responsible and aims to supply him with the means of satisfying his needs through work. It consists of instructing, advising, and reporting because information about performance is a powerful incentive to succeed.

SUMMARY

We began by looking at the psychological needs which should be met if learners are to be motivated to learn efficiently. We then examined the process of communication and found that it comprised non-verbal and verbal components each of which could lead to ambiguity and antagonism or clarity and co-operation. We looked particularly at the process of coping with verbal messages and the hazards associated with them and concluded that the least opportunity for error existed where discussion and feedback gave opportunities for students to check the validity of their decisions; we concluded by pointing to the need for collaborative communication.

REFERENCES

1. Russell, Bertrand, *Authority and the Individual,* George Allen & Unwin, London 1949.
2. Herzberg, F., *Work and the Nature of Man,* Staples Press, London 1968.
3. Emery, F. E. & Thorsrud, Einar, *Form and Content in Industrial Democracy,* Tavistock 1969.
4. European Research Consultants Ltd., *Report on Books and Reading Habits,* London 1965.
5. College Students can be tested with the *Nelson-Denny Reading Test,* Houghton Mifflin Co., Boston 1960 or the *California Reading Vocabulary and Reading Comprehensive Tests, California Test Bureau,* McGraw-Hill, California 1963.

Films

ONE-WAY COMMUNICATION

Watch the film a number of times and select two occasions when the teacher is giving new information; write them down. Note the number of repetitions of this information and the number of non-verbal signals.

Giving new Information about			
No. of repetitions			
No. of Emphases with eyes			
No. of Emphases with hands			

Discuss your findings.

TWO-WAY COMMUNICATION

Watch the film a number of times, observe the teacher and one student, and write down the time in seconds devoted to each activity listed below.

Teacher Time	informing	observing	questioning	encouraging	criticizing
Student Time	passive	listening	informing	answering	questioning

Discuss your findings.

Unit 2

Study Session

Behavioural objectives

AIMS AND OBJECTIVES

In teaching there are aims and objectives and there are behavioural objectives. An aim is a long term end which is usually expressed in fairly general terms. It is sometimes, as it should be, the expression of a philosophy in terms of a course and it is sometimes, as it should not be, an excuse for woolly ineptitude. Here, for example, is an example of an aim.

Aim   To enable students to acquire an understanding of scientific data and to help them to develop a scientific attitude through guided discovery learning.

An objective is more clearcut but it may still lack definition and precision. It describes an intention.

Objective   To teach Ohm's law.

The trouble with this kind of objective is that although it is reasonably precise we would be hard pressed to say what level of learning was intended and therefore whether it had been achieved or not. It is really the teacher's objective for himself. Even if he goes through all the right actions of teaching Ohm's law, he will hardly have taught it to his students' satisfaction if they fail to learn it.

And suppose they do learn it, what does that mean? It may mean that they can recite the law, or write down $I = V/R$, or transpose the equation, or solve numerical problems or perform experiments involving Ohm's law. It may mean that they can explain what Ohm's law means and why there are exceptions and qualifications to it. It may mean that every student will be able to do any of these things or that a proportion of them will.

But what about the following objectives?

Objective To teach the history of the Battle of Waterloo or —
Objective Students will be able to enjoy the music of Mozart or —
Objective An appreciation of French wines?

In each of these cases we could not answer the question, 'How, exactly, do you know whether or not you have achieved your objective?'

BEHAVIOURAL OBJECTIVES

When we learn anything at all we become able to respond to people and situations differently from the way we did before. A boy who discovers a new brand of chocolate has learned; if he tastes it he has learned more; if he buys it he has learned more still. We can tell that he has learned by observing his behaviour — by the way he talks about brands of chocolate, the way he discriminates between the varieties and the look on his face *before* he puts the chocolate in his mouth. Learning is a change in behaviour.

We can tell whether a person has learned this or that only by his behaviour. What he says in answer to the question, 'What are the roots of $x^2 + 3x + 2 = 0$?'. Or what he does when he is asked to drive a car, and so on, tells us whether he has learned or not. Consequently when we plan learning experiences the first question we should ask is, 'What change do I want to cause in the behaviour of my students?' In other words we state our behavioural objectives.

In some circumstances it is very difficult to do this. For example, what should we state as a behavioural objective when teaching students to appreciate the music of Mozart? And yet if they are no different whatever as a consequence of our teaching we have wasted everyone's time. If we teach and as a consequence students learn, a change occurs and we should attempt

to predict that change in order to be able to monitor it respon-
sibly. Statements of behavioural objectives will therefore imply
action: students will be able to *solve* quadratic equations or
solder these joints or *indicate that they recognize* music by
Mozart.

Of course, general objectives of this kind lack precision since
they give neither the conditions under which these abilities
could be demonstrated nor the standards to which they should
be performed. Consequently every statement of objectives
should, ideally, include both conditions and standards (Fig. 6).

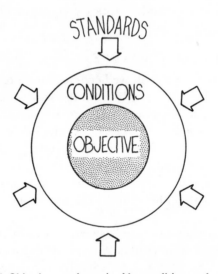

Fig. 6 Objectives are determined by conditions and standards

For example:
   Using an electric soldering bit of his choice, he will be able to
   soft-solder together ten pairs of No. 4 test pieces in ten
   minutes or less, so that the joints cannot be pulled apart by
   hand and so that no solder runs more than 1 mm from the
   joint.

Here,
   the objective is to be able to soft-solder;
   the conditions are that he will use an electric soldering bit and

No. 4 test pieces;

the standard gives an upper limit to the rate at which he does the work, a lower limit to the strength of the joint and a limit to the run of the solder.

As a second example:

He will be able to produce a written translation of any one page of this book from English into French without the use of a dictionary and making fewer than ten errors in less than ten minutes.

LEVELS OF BEHAVIOURAL OBJECTIVES

In preparing behavioural objectives an attempt should be made to indicate the level at which the subject will be known. In the process of cognitive learning, understanding begins with being able to recall some of the information relevant to the subject and ends with being able to make informed judgements within the subject area. Thus a beginner might begin by knowing the definitions of idealism and pragmatism: the philosopher would be able to make critical comparisons of say, educational aims in terms of these philosophies.

The grades of level of cognitive learning may be indicated from answers to the following questions:

Can he recall data or definitions?

Can he use this remembered information to solve specific problems?

Can he break down what he knows to produce a coherent and reliable explanation of what he knows?

Can he use what he knows in new situations and thus extend his knowledge?

Can he make valid and reliable judgements based upon his knowledge?

To take a specific example:

Can he recall the statement of Ohm's law?

Can he find the values of resistances using Ohm's law?

Can he explain how such a relationship could be anticipated in the light of the atomic structure of matter?

27

Can he use what he knows to explain or anticipate the process of conduction in a discharge tube?

Can he argue the relative validity of Ohm's original work against, say, an ammeter—quadrant electrometer method of establishing the law?

The levels of the psychomoter learning of skills follows a similar sequence. A skill may be known to the level of:

Perception — when the skill is known as a series of moves and adjustments: in other words, it has been observed and mentally noted.

Guided response — when the skill can be performed sequentially provided the moves are monitored externally.

Mechanism — when the skill is performed wholly and effectively as a chained sequence of actions.

Evaluation — when the skill is part of a repertoire of skills and is selected to suit particular external conditions and internal preferences.

And finally for affective learning the levels could be:

Attention — noticing and observing.

Response -- taking notice to the stage of seeking meaning.

Valuing — organizing a response among other subjective experiences.

Judging — making evaluation based on a repertoire of experiences.

Whilst it is unrealistic to make extensive definitions of behavioural objectives, these levels should be recognized when the objectives are qualified.

As an example discuss the following objectives:

1. The student will understand how to solve quadratic equations.
2. Every student, without hesitation, will recall the general equation for the roots of $ax^2 + bx + c = 0$.
3. The students will learn to enjoy Mahler's First Symphony.
4. At least half of the group, within the next two weeks, and without any overt persuasion, will ask to borrow a recording of Mahler's First Symphony and listen to it.

Exercise

Write a behavioural objective for a short talk to your group. The subject will be of your own choice and will constitute the objective of the talk you will give in Unit Eight. The objective should have written into it, both conditions and standards, and should be appropriate to your own group.

Be prepared to support your choice of objective if challenged to do so by the group.

Micro-training

Prepare the closing sentence of a talk which you will give to your group in Unit Eight. The talk will have lasted for 15 minutes and will be designed to satisfy the behavioural objective you have just prepared.

For this exercise, although it may be altered for the talk, the sentence should begin with the words: 'You can now', followed by a word such as 'do', 'solve', 'make', 'answer', 'write', 'say', and so on.

Since this is the last thing you say to the group you should feel yourself to be taking your leave of each group member. This impression can be given by looking at everyone in turn, by giving additional weight to the words you use and, if you can rise to it, by looking as though you have enjoyed their company.

If possible these very short presentations will be recorded on video-tape and played back immediately. Discussion should be limited to statements of the most successful aspects of the presentation. Particular attention should be paid to the use of the eyes: during this sentence they should never leave the group and should acknowledge every group member.

Exercise

Closing a talk

1. Select one of the video-taped presentations for special appraisal. Look at it a sufficient number of times to be able to write down the words that seem to you to be given the greatest emphasis.

2. Look at the video again and write down the non-visual support given to this statement as shown in the example:

Statement	And	you	must	never
Voice				slower:
Eyes		fixing students		
Movement			head:	right

forget	that	the	knife	must
intonation				pace:
		looking at knife	fixing	
hand		displaying knife		

pivot	on	its	rounded	end
emphasis			intonation	
students			looking at knife	smiling
			pointing	

3. Write down what you suppose to be the objective of this talk.

4. Discuss your findings.

Unit 3

Study Session

Testing and assessing

Without information about the consequences of our teaching it is virtually impossible to teach at all. Indeed, in the first unit we found that some feedback was essential even to quite trivial communication. For truly efficient teaching we need more than conversational feedback; we need periodical information from which we can adjust the standards and methods of our teaching in strategic terms and also a constant flow of information against which we can make wise tactical refinements.

In the longest term, the effectiveness of our work can be judged only against the kind of persons our students choose to become and the kind of society they choose to make, but in more realistic terms we need assessments which perform two functions:

1. Monitor the student's progress.
2. Measure the terminal effect of our teaching.

Monitoring progress becomes increasingly difficult as the learning becomes more complicated. It is pretty easy, for example, to test our progress when we teach a dog to sit, it is more difficult when we teach a baby to use a spoon and very difficult indeed when we teach a student analytical chemistry.

Terminal tests are usually used for selection purposes either for further courses or for applying the learning in work situations. Basic to any assessment is a decision about priorities since the student's priorities will usually reflect those which are implicit in the testing despite what his teacher may tell him to the contrary. Thus, if, in teaching mathematics, we place the greatest score on getting correct answers, a clever student might simply buy an answer book or choose a good mathematician as his friend. Consequently before testing it is wise to decide what is:

(a) critical

(b) important

and (c) relevant

to the student's thorough mastery of what we are teaching.

Furthermore, any tests we prepare should have three qualities. They should be:

(a) *valid:*   high ratings in the test should correspond to high performance;

(b) *reliable:*   they should give the same result for two equally good candidates or the same result with the same candidate tested twice and having no intervening practice;

(c) *useable.*

The most obvious way of finding out if a student understands something is to ask him to explain it. Simply asking him if he understands it may be useless since it tests a whole complex of pressures — if he is too honest he may play safe and say that he does not, if he cannot stand the teacher's voice he may say he does, and so on. So this will not do. Good verbal teaching is usually a progression of dialogue punctuated by questions which demand more than monosyllabic replies to them.

Of course, students forget what they have learned from one lesson to the next and so many lessons can begin with a question and answer session designed to discover a sound starting point and to establish the importance of accurate recall. Such questioning may be spoken, or written but should generally be brief and pleasurable. Similarly, the end of a lesson usually involves a recapitulatory phase which, again, can usefully take the form of structured questioning.

ESSAY-TYPE QUESTIONS

Questions which call for an essay-type answer test more than the subject matter knowledge called for by the question itself. They require at least the ability to read and write and in certain circumstances such questions would be clearly ridiculous. For example, to ask a child of four to write an answer to the question, 'Describe how to walk', is recognizably inept as a means of discovering his ability as a walker. Regrettably, similarly unwise tests are set from time to time particularly in the testing of craft skills.

Where students should learn to express themselves in essay fashion, such questions have a place, but the inferences drawn from answers need very careful analysis. In 1936, Hartog and Rhodes[1] presented detailed evidence of the unreliability of the marking of examination papers. They showed, for example, that not only do marks for the same paper vary from one examiner to another — sometimes very widely — but they also vary when the same examiner, unknowingly marks the same examination paper on two occasions. Marking calls for a fair measure of modesty.

OBJECTIVE TYPE QUESTIONS

Those tests which, given an answer sheet, can be marked by anyone, to give the same score are called objective tests. Thus the question which says, 'Write the missing date in the following sentence — The Battle of Hastings was fought in the year . . . .' will be answered correctly or incorrectly, whereas the question 'Describe the Battle of Hastings' would never be totally correct and only rarely would it be totally incorrect.

Objective-type tests have other advantages. They seem fair to the students, they can test a wide range of material in a short time and they can be marked very quickly by using a suitable answer sheet.

In general there are three types of objective test. The first requires the student to make up part of a sentence — perhaps only a single word will do — but since he chooses what to write such a test is called a *constructed response* type test. An example would be:

Complete the following sentence —

An internal combustion engine is so called because the fuel to drive it is_____.

33

This type of question tests what a student actually knows about the subject.

The second type requires the student to remember something and is consequently called a *recall* type test. An example would be:

An_____engine is so called because the fuel to drive it is burned inside its cylinders.

The third type asks students to choose one or more correct answers among a number of right and wrong alternatives. This is called a recognition type test and has value in, not only testing, but also in assisting and reinforcing recall. An example of this type of test would be:

Cross out the wrong statement in the following sentence —

A $\begin{matrix} \text{motor car petrol engine} \\ \text{steam turbine engine} \end{matrix}$ is an internal combustion engine.

Of course, it is often so easy to guess the correct one of two alternatives that three alternatives would be better, thus:

Cross out the one or two incorrect statements in the following sentence —

A $\begin{matrix} \text{motor car petrol engine} \\ \text{jet aircraft engine} \\ \text{steam turbine engine} \end{matrix}$ is an internal combustion engine;

or write down the following words correctly arranged —

Chien	Head
Assiette	Dog
Bras	Chair
Tête	Plate
Chaise	Arm

The following further examples of objective tests are all taken from physics.

CONSTRUCTED RESPONSE TYPE QUESTIONS – TEST KNOWLEDGE

Complete the following sentences:

(a) The pressure at a depth of 10m is greater in sea water than in fresh water because _____.

(b) The centre of gravity of a cycle wheel will not be on the centre line of its axle because_____.

(c) The sum of three non-parallel forces which do not meet in a point can always be represented by a single force and _____.

RECALL TYPE QUESTION – TEST MEMORY

(a) 1 volt = 1_____per coulomb.
(b) The direction of current induced in a circuit is such as to _____ the change producing it.
(c) The minimum instantaneous value of an alternating e.m.f. is equal to_____.

RECOGNITION TYPE QUESTIONS – CONTRIBUTE TO LEARNING

Cross out the one or two incorrect alternatives in each group below.

(a) The product of a force and a distance may give
    work done
    torque
    power.

(b) Two iron weights, one ten times as heavy as the other, fall from the same height to the ground. The temperature of the heavy one will rise about
    the same amount
    ten times as much
    a tenth as much
    as that of the light one.

(c) Alternating current can be used for
    electroplating
    heating
    driving electric motors.

Each item in the following list on the left is equal to one or more items on the right. Decide which, and put its letter in the space provided. Number one on the right has been completed.

(a) Coefficient of friction	3,600,000 joules	(g)
(b) Pressure	joule	_____
(c) Force	force per unit area	_____
(d) Momentum	mass × acceleration	_____
(e) Unit of angular displacement	newton-metre	_____
(f) One joule per second	1 watt	_____
(g) One kilowatt-hour	F/R	_____
	radian	_____
	mass × velocity	_____

Some qualities are a complex of such a wide variety of factors that it is impossible to measure them objectively. For example, it would be quite impossible to measure with absolute certainty a man's ability to teach, even though there is remarkable agreement as to who is a good teacher and who is a bad one. In such cases, scales with written explanation of their gradings can be useful — these are called verbalized rating scales.

Such a scale might be used in assessing qualities such as persistence, concentration and initiative — two examples are given below:

Mark on the following scale the point corresponding to the student's —

PERSISTENCE

Gives up completely at first difficulty.	Restless and frequently distracted.	Works steadily but easily stopped.	Not easily stopped.	Concentrates intensely and stops only when told to so so.

A more fully developed set of such rating scales is given below. This shows a proposed assessment sheet for the use of aircraft captains in reporting on the competencies of trainee pilots under their command.

CAPTAIN'S CONFIDENTIAL CREW REPORT

Please mark on the scales given, the closest measure of your assessment. If you are *particularly* unsure of the measure, mark on either side of your preferred decision the range within which you are certain the assessment would lie — mark these with a letter o as shown:

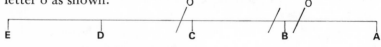

E	D	C	B	A

1. If you learned that this officer was to make the next twenty voyages with you, you would react to the news:
   A. with conscious pleasure and anticipation.
   B. with satisfaction.
   C. as news.

D. by wishing that it could have been another officer for reasons that can be expressed in words.

E. with anxiety or irritation.

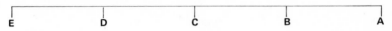

2. Piloting skill

A. he made no error of judgement and at no time did you feel he was likely to do so.

B. he made no error of judgement that could be expressed in words but you occasionally felt that he might do so.

C. he demonstrated the degree of skill that you expect from men with his experience.

D. he made some errors of judgement that can be expressed in words. These made you doubt either his competency or training.

E. you would not allow members of your family to fly as his passengers.

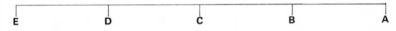

3. Technical and Operational Knowledge

A. he knows as much as you do.

B. he made no mistakes but you are sure he knows less than you do.

C. he knows as much as you would expect of someone with his experience.

D. he displayed ignorance, examples of which can be expressed in words.

E. his knowledge would have been insufficient for the safety of the aircraft if you had died.

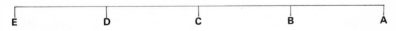

4. Command Potential

A. if he assumed command now he would display all the qualities of our best pilots.

B. if he assumed command now he would in no way betray his lack of command experience.

C. if he assumed command now he would be acceptable to his passengers and crew.

D. he is not ready for command for reasons that can be expressed in words but he will be ready later on.

E. he lacks one quality necessary to command. This to be taken from the point of view of one of the following:
(a) passengers (b) the company (c) cabin staff (d) flight deck crew.

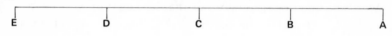

5. Statement

If any one of the assessments are nearer to D than any other mark, please express in words ONE of these assessments.

If 4 is marked E state the quality that is lacking and from whose point of view this is of consequence.

GRADING

Reliable assessments, in general, should give a spread of marks which follow a normal distribution pattern (Fig. 7). For every 100 students tested the pattern of competency should be very roughly:

    2 outstanding
    23 good
    50 average
    23 weak
    2 fail

This does not mean that of 100 students taking an externally set examination 2 *should* fail: indeed this would be remarkable. It means that provided the level of the course is matched to the student intake, the testing procedures used by the teacher should give this kind of distribution even if the two called 'fail' are brilliantly successful: they would simply be 'fail' relative to the 50 'average' students.

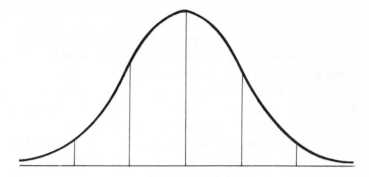

Fig. 7 A normal distribution curve

SUMMARY

Assessment aims at (a) monitoring progress;
 (b) terminal testing.
Assessment should imply the aspects of competency which are
regarded as: (a) critical;
 (b) important;
 (c) relevant.
Tests should be: (a) valid;
 (b) reliable;
 (c) useable.
Essay-type questions test more than subject knowledge.
Objective questions may be of the following types:
  (a) constructed response (to test knowledge);
  (b) recall (to test memory);
  (c) recognition (to test progress).

Subjective measures may be more reliable if they are made on
verbalized rating scales.
 The distribution of the marks of a group should be normal.

REFERENCE

1. Hartog, Sir P., and Rhodes, E. C., *Examination of Examinations,*
 Macmillan, London 1936.

Exercise

1. Prepare an objective-type test to measure the effectiveness of the talk you intend to give in Unit Eight. This should be duplicated prior to the talk.

2. Each group member will give a short talk as a micro-training exercise. Read the requirement for this given below and prepare a verbalized rating scale with which you can give an assessment of a speaker's success in establishing rapport. Discuss these scales and prepare an agreed scale from them. Duplicate this agreed scale for use in the micro-training exercise.

Micro-training
Establishing rapport

A group of disabled elderly people are to be entertained by your students just before Christmas. They are sitting in your college hall and you are to make a short speech of welcome. As you do so you try to make them feel at ease.

Prepare and present such a short talk of two or three minutes duration designed to make these guests feel at home.

Each group member will mark his rating scale and give it to each speaker in turn.

Film
Rapport

Watch the film a number of times and select the one characteristic that, in your view, contributes most effectively to rapport.

Discuss your view with the rest of the group.

Unit 4

Study Session
Managing a discussion

The objective of this first section is to be responsible for what goes on when a group of people are able to talk freely. This skill underlies discussion leading, seminar leading and, to an extent, holding a tutorial.

The exercise may appear to the 'experts' to be too leader centred but we feel that the ability to predict outcomes and the discipline of unobtrusive control are prerequisites of the more difficult task of giving value through greater freedom. Without this background, discussion periods and seminars can be distructive and even frightening experiences.

PEOPLE WORKING TOGETHER

A discussion is not a debate: it is a collaborative exercise in which people's knowledge and experience is shared in such a way that it becomes refined, enhanced and appreciated. There cannot be discussion of facts; facts are known or not known, they can be stated or ignored. Discussion centres upon concepts and feelings, upon the reliability of what we believe we understand, upon the wisdom or folly of decisions, upon attitudes and prejudices.

When people are in conflict they are expressing the driving forces that lie behind their actions and the emotional goals in their lives; their feelings of pride or fear. When we lead or participate in a discussion, the more we understand other people, the more sensitive we are to their drives and feelings, the less frustrated we feel about ideas that seem irrational from our point of view.

During discussion, whether it centres on topics of universal human concern such as family relationships or of specialized knowledge such as the meaning of the word 'energy', people will express their need for friends, for leadership, for ways to earn approval and to work off frustration, ways to feel persons of consequence and to avoid feeling foolish. The teacher's fundamental professional concern as he participates in every discussion with his students whether it be formally or informally is to recognize the humanness of every individual and his need for ego-support and to act to prevent demoralization. The essence of good discussion is the conflict of ideas and either their resolution or the informed recognition of their differences.

During discussion, group members will be exposed to one another's points of view, to alternative interpretations. This is most important when the group is dealing with ambiguous situations. This occurs, for example, in liberal studies, where the discussion of a moral dilemma may introduce the members to ways of looking at the problem which would never have occurred to them. It may also give them an opportunity to put their own points of view to a hard critical scrutiny by the other participants in the discussion.

A discussion should motivate students through social recognition and group success: it should be so managed that each member feels a personal responsibility for every other member: it should aim at replacing a 'pecking order' by a group spirit. And since every group member should feel he has an opportunity of contributing, the group size should not exceed eleven or twelve.

OBJECTIVES

Some would have it that we can teach *new* knowledge through discussion but, if this happens at all, it happens only in the hands of extraordinary enthusiasts: faith can move mountains — it also sustains the Magic Circle. In general, discussion is useful for:

(a) refining and structuring concepts so that they become

more reliable and consequentially more useful. For example, the concept of an electric current which may begin by resembling a flow of water could assume a form more useful for problem solving in electronic circuitry and the concept of honesty could be refined by hearing other experiences and interpretations.

(b) analysing 'procedures, organizations and functions'. For instance, the most effective way of running a laboratory might be found by discussing the problem with students and technicians.

(c) examining the applicability of general principles to particular circumstances. For example, given certain principles and constraints how would we, as store managers, cope with shoplifting.

(d) recapitulation and revision of learning experiences such as projects, visits, lectures and conferences.

(e) exposing, comparing and examining attitudes. This may harden an undesirable attitude, but at least it broadens the base upon which future ideas will be structured.

When the objective is primarily concerned with knowledge or with the orientation of attitudes to conform to a pre-determined pattern (punctuality is important: ostracizing coloured people is bad), the discussion should be formal, in which case it needs direction and preparation and the leader must be thoroughly briefed. It may, for example, complement other learning by following a lecture.

An unled discussion group of inexperienced students often throws up its own leader and, having done so, tends to over-depend on him and although such groups may reach valuable, sensible and humane conclusions they can readily reach conclusions which are socially unacceptable, technically unrealistic and intellectually ridiculous. Not only this, but since such conclusions are the result of their unaided creative abilities, they assume a disproportionate importance in the minds of the participants.

However, in view of the nature of discussion, students must feel free to express what they actually want to express. If, in his anxiety to stimulate contributions, the teacher seems relieved and pleased with observations, however irrelevant or useless they may be, he will put a premium upon talking for its own sake and will tend to encourage chatter at the expense of serious thinking. On the other hand, if he entirely dismisses irrelevant observations he may dismiss both co-operation and important and valuable ideas which lie buried beneath the inept statements. At all times he must look for the reasons which lie behind contributions since once he has understood he can help his students either to express themselves more lucidly or to revise their ideas.

PREPARATION

A discussion, generally speaking, needs preparation. The leader should begin by deciding with some precision why he intends to have a discussion and in what ways it contributes to the needs of the group: he should know his objective.

Next he should assemble the facts which bear upon the subject: if they consist of tables of data these will need duplicating and distributing in advance but otherwise they will be included in the leader's introduction. He may also include the points of view of people of consequence so long as these are unlikely to stifle the students' contributions. For example, a discussion of the nature of light might be introduced by a historical summary of ideas on the subject including, for example, Newton's corpuscular theory. This gives psychological support to the student who holds outmoded views for which there is nevertheless powerful, if insufficient evidence.

He should then choose the sequence of sub-headings which are likely to be most helpful in the light of the abilities, interests and attitudes of the group and he should jot down his plan. This lends precision to the exercise.

The leader's plan then consists of:
1. Objective.
2. Outline introduction containing relevant facts.
3. Headings under which the discussion will proceed.

Finally, the leader should check the facilities and prepare any material he needs and arrange the seating so that it is roughly in the form of a circle (Fig. 8). It is best if no person, particularly the leader, has a special seat or a special position since everyone should be able to look at everyone else and feel equally provided for.

PROCEDURE

A formal discussion opens with the leader introducing the topic in such a way that everyone can note the relevant facts, and knows precisely why he is to be engaged in the exercise. The leader may, indeed, write information on a chalkboard or flip-chart.

Fig. 8 A discussion group

Next he may outline the headings under which the discussion will proceed and, in any case, he will usually present the opening topic in the form of a question and then wait for a response. This waiting period is critical, for if he appears anxious for a contribution he will tend to promote superficiality rather than reflexion.

When contributions are made, he should let ideas move around the group, asking for clarification if it is necessary, and making the least number of interventions to keep the contributions relevant. His major preoccupation will be in understanding why individuals say what they do and then in helping them in the light of this understanding. At the end of each stage he will summarize the discussion so far, and give credit for especially helpful statements. Most important he will take away information about the scope and level of understanding displayed by the group members and then use this information in preparing his subsequent teaching.

SUMMARY

Discussion is a sharing of ideas, a resolution of conflicting ideas or a recognition of other points of view. It aims at deepening understanding and encouraging co-operative learning. It is useful for concept structuring, analysing procedures, examining particular ideas in the light of principles and recapitulating earlier learning.

A discussion should be prepared in advance.

Members should feel equally provided for.

Discussion should be used as an opportunity for self-assessment by the teacher.

Exercise
Preparation of a discussion

Each group member to prepare a discussion to be conducted in Unit Five. The topic should be of general interest such as:

'Saving schemes for the small investor.'
'Insuring a car (home).'
'Correspondence courses and the Open University.'
'Preparation for retirement.'
'Alcoholism.'
'Coffee mornings.'
'Nursery schools.'
'The colour problem.'

Micro-training
Opening a discussion

Each group member to present to the group the opening of the discussion he has prepared. If possible, this should be videotaped and played back immediately it has been given.

The opening should begin with a precise statement of the objective of the discussion, the necessary facts of the case and the headings under which the discussion will develop; it should be brief.

The presentations should be commented on in relation to the following:
1. Were the non-verbal signals relevant and useful?
2. Was the objective stated clearly and precisely?
3. Did the factual statements sound like facts or opinions?
4. Was the proposed development helpful?

Each group member should, for each presentation, fill in the following rating scales; the position and scatter of his markings will indicate the progress the group is making.

INTRODUCTION (OBJECTIVE)

I was totally confused.	I felt unsure about the objective.	I needed some clarification about what I could usefully say.	I knew the objective but had reservations about my role.	I knew exactly what was required of me.

INTRODUCTION (MOTIVATION)

I felt apathetic.	I was willing to participate.	I was interested.	I wanted to contribute and to hear others.	I felt totally involved.

Film
Managing a discussion

Watch the film at least three times. Observe the leader and make a note of the approximate time he spends in the following activities. Discuss your findings.

Giving information	
Receiving information	
Reinforcing ideas	
Discouraging ideas	
Bringing in	
Terminating	

This kind of observation requires much practice. One technique is to make a stroke every second and when four strokes have been made cross them out for the fifth and then start again, thus:

~~IIII~~   ~~IIII~~   11 = (12 seconds)

The skill in doing this lies in making the strokes automatically whilst paying full attention to the film.

Unit 5

Practical Exercise

Leading a discussion

Each group member will lead, for fifteen minutes duration, the discussion he has prepared in *Unit Four*. At the end of each discussion members will fill in the verbalized rating scales which they prepared in *Unit Three* and then give them to the leader.

The leader, having read the scales, will seek suggestions and advice from those members who have been less than completely satisfied with his performance.

The scales should not be in evidence during the discussion. The tutor might complete part of the following analysis as a guide to his summing up.

Leading a discussion

CONTENT

Time (min.)	0	1	2	3	4	5	6	7	8	9	10	11	12	13	14	15
Leader talking																
Group members talking to leader																
Group members talking to group																

AN INDUCTION COURSE

LEADER QUESTIONING

Probing questioning	
Higher order questioning	
Divergent questioning	

NON-VERBAL CUEING

Eyes	
Pause	
Movement	

REINFORCING

Non-verbal	
Verbal	

Opening   Information _____

              Motivation _____

Close   Precision in Summarizing _____

              Effectiveness of Reinforcement _____

Module II

Talking to students

and other matters

Unit 6

FACTORS WHICH INFLUENCE LEARNING

Learning — its content, efficiency and permanency — is affected by a wide spectrum of factors, many of which are highly individual. In this course we divide the topic into three main areas under the general headings of perception, adolescence and psychology. The divisions are to be taken as matters of time-tabling and not as indicative of any discontinuity.

PERCEPTION

Perceiving is a mental activity in which one reaches out for an interpretation of the sensory impressions received from outside through the senses of vision, hearing, tasting, feeling and smelling. In other words, perception is an *active* response to communication. So long as we are conscious we are constantly receiving a vast stream of information about the nature of our environment, but rather than attempt to cope with it all, we choose particular items. Thus the first stage in perception is attention to particular stimuli (Fig. 9).

ATTENTION

The interesting characteristic of attention is its degree of selectivity: we attend to only one aspect of what we decide is most important at any given time. Thus, if a teacher is interesting enough, a student will disregard the noise and views outside of the classroom window and attend to, say, his words, or his voice, or what he is saying. We can test the fact that generally we can attend to only·one thing at a time by trying to hold a conversation while a television set is turned on. What happens is that we attend to some of the conversation and in between try to catch occasional words from the set to find out what the programme is about. If the speaker is a great deal more interesting than the programme, we may block out what is happening on the television, but at any instant we will attend to one or the other — we cannot focus simultaneously on both.

Fig. 9 Attention leads to perception

Similarly, when people claim that they can read or study only when there is a background noise it does not imply that they are capable of listening and studying at the same time. What it generally means is that total silence is more distracting to them than having, say, music playing in the background because during absolute silence, they actually start listening — for odd sounds perhaps — and because they give their attention to listening they cannot give it to studying.

Attention, then, is a selective focusing of the mind upon a target and as teachers we must be constantly aware of possible distractions to this focusing. For instance, it is prudent to ensure that all visual material including the chalkboard carries only as much information as is relevant to our teaching at the moment.

However, the duration of closely focused attention is brief: the film-maker reckons it to be only eleven seconds. Our attention is constantly shifting from its main focus, first to one point and then to another and in doing so, if we go on 'attending' to the central theme, we receive clues and other information relevant to this focus. When, for instance, we 'attend to' a work of art we first scan it rather superficially in order to acquire a vague general idea of its total content. We may then focus for a while on one particular part — the central figure perhaps — that interests us specially and although we may many times return to that one special focal point, our eyes are constantly moving away from it to take in other information and provide our main interest with more significance.

If, however, we *fix* our attention on one black spot in the middle of a piece of paper, it seems as though once the satiation point is passed our perception becomes distorted and the spot may seem to 'move' or take on a different shape or colour. Failing this, although we continue to gaze on the dot, our minds start wandering and we find it impossible to concentrate exclusively on the dot. This same part-hypnotic state can be induced by a teacher if he overemphasizes details.

Now, if that dot *were* to move, we would start predicting further moves and attempt to create a pattern out of the moves the dot made. If the dot were to move from side to side like a pendulum, in the absence of other sensory stimuli, we might well find ourselves lulled into an almost soporific state. This tends to happen when a teacher talks with a droning monotony or when he throws chalk up and down rhythmically, or sways to and fro as he teaches.

If we try to attend visually to a large number of objects simultaneously, this focus shifting occurs until we have the whole picture fitting together into some sort of mental pattern: only after this will we be able to take in each separate item at a time (Fig. 10). So that the greater the amount of detail given at one time the more difficult it is to study separate components satisfactorily. But the value of this shifting focus phenomenon is

Fig. 10 A picture without a theme

that it enables us to group objects together into some sort of pattern so that we learn about components by the company they keep. To satisfy both these learning needs we resort to such procedures as showing first a block schematic diagram to give a general pattern of the whole and then making a detailed study of each block in turn (Fig. 11), or by regarding the human body as skeleton + muscles + digestive system and so on in a broad general way and then studying each separately and relating it back to the whole.

A similar process goes on when we attend to other sensory impressions. When we listen to someone talking we take in groups of words and only afterwards — often too late — do we attend to individual words. For this reason, difficult words or

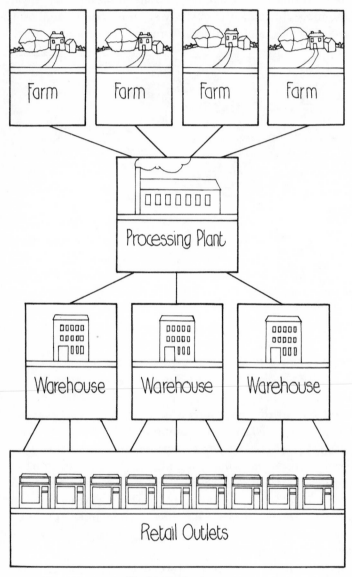

Fig. 11 Block schemata

technical words should be repeated at the end of the sentence which contains them.

One other aspect of attention should be recognized. Just as a hungry man is irresistibly drawn to pictures of food, so in a class-room students may squander their attention on irrelevant details simply because of their own particular physical or emotional needs at that time. Good teachers are prepared for this kind of inattention to lessons and make humane allowances for it.

INTERPRETATION

Without attention, perception, and hence learning will not happen. So attention must be planned for, and so far as possible, understood. Perception, as has been said, is the *active* interpreta-tion of sensory impressions, but in order to be able to interpret and identify sensations, there must have been some previous learning. For example, in order for us to know that a certain metal object is a gyroscope there must have been a first occasion when we were told that this was indeed, a gyroscope. To be able to say it with conviction we must have some knowledge of its function.

In a similar way since a child's very early experience of furry animals is derived from a dog or cat, he will say 'doggy' or 'pussy' when he sees another four-legged furry animal until a separate identity is given to it and he recognizes special qualities in it which do not attach to dogs or cats.

What our perceptual experiences do, in fact, is enable us to build up a world of identifiable objects, and perception takes place when we consciously recognize an experience in terms of this repertoire. This derives from our ability to find in our mental storehouse, similarities, contrasts or contiguities which we then recognize in the context of our emotional, physical and social environment at that time.

Each individual is constantly storing up a mental bank of information about his world which will enable him to perceive later experiences. Thus, we can appreciate that perception depends heavily on the learning that occurs during a child's early formative years from birth to the age of about five. It follows, therefore, that the more experiences a child learns to cope with during his early years, the more he is able to come to terms with his environment later on. Hence the value of pre-school playgroups. It follows that children reared in homes where there are few books and pictures, where there is little opportunity to play with many different things and few toys for them to take apart, are at a positive disadvantage when they start school compared with their more fortunate peers. More-over, these children remain impoverished for a very long time, and however equal their opportunities in formal education may be, they can never quite compensate for this early deprivation.

The way a person learns depends on how he perceives. Although experiences of a physical nature such as sight, sound, taste, touch and smell may well be common ones, the ways we perceive them are often different and unique because our per-ception is special to us — it is idiosyncratic. Thus, if I complain of a headache to someone who has never had one his reaction will be different from that of someone who perpetually suffered from migraine attacks. Moreover, although I can describe the pain in the head from which I suffer and give the listener some idea of the pain, he cannot experience *my* pain.

MOTIVATED PERCEPTION

Our interpretation of the environment then, our perception, is much more than the sensations we receive, it is sensations inter-preted through ideas and images derived from past experiences in the context of our present physical, mental and emotional state. Perception at any moment is therefore likely to be affec-ted by such factors as attitudes and expectation or desire at that moment. Thus, perception is very much guided by our inner feelings and to this extent we may call it 'motivated perception'. An obvious example of this is the phenomenon of the mirage in the desert which is seen as actual water by a very thirsty man. The 'motivated' character of perception accounts too for the variety of interpretations of aesthetic qualities: an erstwhile beautiful woman can look quite unattractive when she is nagging and Beethoven pales during a bilious attack. It is clearly not the woman or the music that has changed, but rather our inner state that has modified our perceptual experience.

It follows that we, as teachers, must be constantly aware of the possible teaching difficulties which these differences create. Consequently when we teach, we would be well advised to use, not only words, but, when they are called for, pictures, objects and a wide variety of communications media, a variety of methods and even a variety of environments in an effort to ensure that this heterogeneous group we call students is well served.

SUMMARY

Perception is the mental coding of those stimuli to which we attend: it is a reaching out after meaning.

The reliability of our perception derives from the quality of our past experiences and our mastery of language.

Perception is moderated by our feelings — motivated perception — and varies with our personal make-up.

We perceive, to a degree, what we want to perceive, what we expect to perceive and what we have previously decided we will perceive.

Teachers should cater for this apparent waywardness by using a variety of methods and media.

Micro-training
Opening a talk

Each group member will present the opening two or three sentences of the talk he intends to give in *Unit Eight*. As he does so he will use non-verbal signals to show he recognizes each of his listeners and he will emphasize the title of the talk by stating it deliberately, pausing and then stating it again with precisely the same intonation. As he states the title he will make some kind of gesture to emphasize it. Video playback will be used if possible.

Each group member will prepare — prior to the exercise — a verbalized rating scale to measure the value of the total emphasis.

Study Session

FACTORS WHICH INFLUENCE LEARNING

2. *Behavioural patterns of adolescence*

SELF-FULFILMENT

It has been said that, 'human life is not merely a perpetual struggle for survival but more, a perpetual struggle for self-fulfilment'.

Although we may be soothed by the charismic profundity of this message we would do well to look into it. What goes for motivation, co-operation, interest, participation and the rest derives in the end from the internal forces that make us want to go on living and being ourselves. In times of hardship the struggle for survival may become an almost irresistible motivation to learn — the achievements of Air Training Corps cadets in the Second World War were astonishing: the diligent struggling through years of nightschool in the Twenties matched only the persistence of the Jarrow hunger marchers.

Now that the need to learn in order to survive is less apparent, the effect of the struggle for self-fulfilment seems greater. To some, it seems to be a desire to realize their potential and to achieve all that is possible within the framework of their ability and environment: to others it seems to be a search for their own identities.

James Hemming, in a lecture to The Faculty of Education of the University College of Swansea, said:

'Self-fulfilment is said to be the consequence of having lived our past sufficiently well for us to prove adequate to our particular present, with its possibilities and problems'.

Thus, to get to school a five year old must have learned to walk and talk, to feed himself and to perform a multiplicity of manual skills. Not only this, he will have learned how to learn before he could learn. In the same way we learn to live before we can be alive, and this bears witness to the notion that there is a sixth, all pervading sense, the sense of being — the self-fulfilment sense.

ADOLESCENCE

During his early school years a child is very much part of various groups — the family, the class, the school, the neighbourhood and so on. As he grows his need to be recognized by others which has hitherto been very much a family affair, now attaches to a group of young people with similar interests and about the same age as himself — his peer group.

This attachment to groups involves him in thinking in group terms and limits expressions of his own individuality. Ultimately acceptance of this group involvement is insufficient to satisfy him and he seeks his own unique identity — this is the stage we have come to call adolescence.

It has been said that adolescence was invented by Jean Jacques Rousseau. His book, *Emile*[1] published in 1762, was probably the first written account of the emotional and moral dilemma with which a young adult is faced. But as a study, adolescence largely escaped the scrutiny of psychologists until the beginning of the present century. In 1904, G. Stanley Hall claimed that adolescence was a 'time of storm and stress' or 'sturm und drang'. Since then, many other workers have attempted to describe, to analyse, to hypothesize and publicize a variety of theories to explain the behaviour patterns of adolescents. But the trouble with theories is that they may create the problems they set out to explain. And for too long we have been persuaded to accept the notion that this period of life is particularly fraught with difficulties. It is encouraging, therefore, to note that contemporary work on the subject is turning more and more towards a scientific approach in which the rather emotive generalizations of the past are avoided.

Now, if we accept that adolescence is a special developmental phase, we should be precise in the way we define it. If, for instance, we regard it as the in-between stage of childhood and maturity then our view is entirely dependent on what we mean by both childhood and maturity. If we say that adolescence starts with the development of puberty, this is fine because we can at least be precise about our definition of puberty: the age at which we are first able to have children. This varies between and within the sexes. For girls, puberty begins with the onset of menstruation or the menarche and the age at which this happens is decreasing. At the beginning of the century it was on average sixteen years, whilst today it is around thirteen years and is not uncommon in eleven and twelve year olds.[2] This particular trend shows no sign of ending and at its present rate, by the year 2000, the average age of menarche could well be nine or ten. And although it is not the purpose of this book to look into the reasons why this trend has occurred, it should remind us that for girls, at any rate, physiological childhood is becoming shorter. For boys, puberty commonly occurs around the fourteenth year with a period of rapid skeletal growth, enlargement of the genital organs and involuntary seminal emission.

So much for the start of adolescence. But when we come to complete our definition of this developmental stage, we find that its termination is not easily explained. If we say that it is concluded when a person matures into an adult, we can find little agreement about either the meanings of mature or of adult, and, what is more some people never seem to mature at all. Margaret Mead in *Growing up in New Guinea*[3] and *Coming of Age in Samoa*[4] found that in some cultures, there was in fact no in-between period at all. The ritual pubertal ceremonies changed the child into an adult overnight: a splendid way of eliminating the 'problem of adolescence'!

At one time, we in Britain decreed that an individual was considered truly adult at the age of twenty-one and was officially given adult status at that age, now the age of social adulthood is eighteen. And if it were to suit our culture in some future time, it would be equally easy to make that magic age thirty-five or fifteen. So that as far as a definition is concerned we can do little better than to say that adolescence is a period of development which starts with the onset of physical maturity and ends with the age of social maturity as decided by the society to which we belong.

PHYSICAL DEVELOPMENT

We have already mentioned that the most significant physical characteristic of adolescence is the onset of puberty. This occurs when the gonadotrophic hormones are secreted in sufficiently large quantities to bring about maturity of the sex glands. It is accompanied by a variety of other physical characteristics which may or may not play an important part in behaviour.

Here, we should mention the theories which link hormonal influences with emotional and even intellectual processes. Recent studies, for example, show a quite dramatic falling off in the level of mental concentration in girls for two days before and after menstruation. One study conducted in secondary schools showed that girls who sat examinations during this period were less likely to do as well as they might at any other time. And although many studies are inconclusive we must believe that hormonal influences on adolescents can be considerable.

Adolescence is also a period of rapid skeletal growth. From the age of eleven to sixteen the bones go through the period of ossification and grow to their full. Some studies have shown that the period of maximum growth takes place during the year in which puberty occurs and try to link this fact with the increasing clumsiness of adolescents at this time. However, most studies show, in fact, that there is minimal loss of manual dexterity during this period.

Also, at this time, there are skin changes most commonly occurring in boys but by no means uncommon in girls. Skin eruptions such as acne are the commonest complaints and so far almost resistant to treatment. To the young person, struggling to achieve some sort of ego identity and becoming more and more aware of his bodily functions, conditions of this sort cause not only physical discomfort but often lead to a feeling of inferiority and even utter despondency. Feelings of self-consciousness and inferiority can also be experienced by a person who reaches puberty either at an abnormally early age or an abnormally late age and such feelings may well cause abnormal behaviour such as school refusal or deliquency, if not handled by both teachers and parents in an understanding but sympathetic manner.

SOCIAL DEVELOPMENT OF ADOLESCENTS

During the first five years of life a child is almost completely dependent on his parents and siblings. Nursery school and primary school continue the socialization process, but still the child tends to cling to his parents and demonstrates a reluctance to spend any great time away from them. Gradually, over the years, the child becomes more adventurous and begins to form friendships in the neighbourhood. These friendships are often of short duration and fraught with quarrels, and with each setback the child returns to the comfort of his home. During these early years he is not able to cope with the give and take of more mature friendships, there is an egocentricity which renders him unable to see situations from another person's point of view. It is not until he reaches his teens that he makes definite attempts to break away from this pattern: he starts questioning the authority of his parents, he starts to form stronger friendships outside his home and quite often his friends tend to be those who would not normally be chosen by his parents if they were able to do so. In other words the young adult shows signs of attempting to be independent. The security and warmth he once found in the family unit is now rejected in favour of approval by his peer group and there is a tendency for average adolescents to form groups having a distinct heirarchical pattern of leader and led. And so he turns away from his home and starts adopting the behaviour patterns of his group. His friends will influence his opinions, his attitudes, his way of speaking and his way of dress. Parents, for their part, will commonly complain of feeling at a loss to understand the change in their child. Sometimes a young person may reject completely the standards and values of his family and the parents may react by adopting strong authoritarian attitudes with the imposition of strict and rigid sanctions. The process of growing up can become a struggle against all authority.

Towards the age of thirteen and fourteen, the young person

may develop a strong attachment for someone of the same sex. Freud called this the homosexual phase, and Kinsey in his study of American youth revealed a significant degree of homosexual feelings during adolescence. Later studies have shown that homosexual feelings are less common in co-educational establishments than they are in single sex schools, and although we may feel that this was a predictable enough outcome of such studies, we should remind ourselves that 'homosexual feelings' per se, in no way imply homosexual activity; often a young person feels a sort of hero worship for a member of the same sex with whom he or she can identify. This hero worship develops with age and by the time the young person is sixteen commonly consists of a short-lived and sterile 'romantic' love affair with a 'hero' of the opposite sex.

Gradually, the young person starts assessing the adult world at large; he shows signs of increased introspection and loses his child-like faith in adults: he begins to form his own style of life. In time he starts to make moral judgement of the world, and more important, demonstrates his independence by forming his own values and standards. By the time he is sixteen he has strong ideas of what is right and wrong, he seems to see everything clearly in absolutes so that he may know with certainty that poverty is wrong and capitalism is evil. The world problems could be easily solved if the rich gave to the poor and so on.

This purely idealistic phase is commonly seen as the young person's search for his real self, or the search for ego-identification. Very often he looks at the adult world, and does not much like what he sees: there is injustice and intolerance, there is cruelty and persecution, and yet somewhere he has to find a niche for himself, an individual in his own right. He wants desperately to change the world, or to make an impact; he feels that the adults do not care enough and that they have become hypnotized into moral apathy, and thus he may become rebellious and angry, determined not to become a part of the vast ignoble plot of a corrupt society, and in this he may be quite uncompromising.

Alternatively, if the adult world seems too brutal and too unfair, he may retreat into his own world of phantasy for comfort and self assurance. Overwhelming feelings of social inadequacy and social impotence may lead him to become trapped by his own phantasies: he may resort to acts of heroism or even become delinquent. And where delinquent acts are conducted by a young person on his own they are seen as a very real and deep-seated emotional disturbance. Further, these cases of individual delinquency often have a common familial background — lack of parental love or fair discipline during this very important time.

INTELLECTUAL DEVELOPMENT OF ADOLESCENTS

As a child grows he passes through a series of pretty well-defined stages of intellectual development. These have been described in detail by Piaget and his co-workers.[5] In further education we are largely concerned with the final stages although the effects of the earlier ones bear upon the latter.

During his first two years of life a child is acquainting himself with a variety of sensory experiences which form the basis of his perceptual ability. In the following four or five years he learns to talk and this enables him to put names to things, to describe them and to relate causes and effects.

After seven he enters what Piaget calls the concrete stage of thinking during which he first becomes aware of his own mental processes. He develops the ability to observe very closely, to collect things in classified groups, to discriminate physical qualities and to separate out criteria for judgement — tall does not necessarily mean big. He is able to understand fractions, speed, temperature and so on, so long as they are not too far removed from his own experience. Some children even become fascinated by the concept of numbers, they are intrigued by the smallest, the greatest, the largest and a few may experiment with the notion of infinity.

After eleven or twelve he *may* enter the formal stage when he can appreciate the relationships between classes of objects, when he can represent them by abstractions and then go on to express relationships between these abstractions. Thus, the Boyle's law relationship $P_1 : P_2$ as $V_2 : V_1$ is meaningful and problems such as 'Dick is taller than Tom and shorter than Bill; who is the tallest?' can be solved without visualizing the objects themselves.

This level leads to a final sophisticated phase of thinking called by Piaget the hypothetico-deductive phase when the relationships between abstractions can be expressed as hypotheses and then tested for their validity, when rational judgements can be made on abstractions which lie outside immediate experience.

For intellectual maturity it is essential to reach the stage of formal thinking since it brings untouched areas of experience into the scope of the intellect, makes reliable judgement possible and reduces our dependence upon a welter of separate items of data. Before this stage it is impossible for a student to understand what science is all about.

However, this development from the concrete stage of thinking to the formal stage varies with individuals and derives from their backgrounds, experiences and opportunities. Primitive people never reach the formal stage[6] and it is not unreasonable to believe that some half of the students in further education need intelligent guidance if they are to reach it before their formal education ends, if at all.

The transition is possible only against a sufficient background of concrete thinking around a central issue — of experience, practical work, demonstration, projects, reading and discussion. Flitting from one theoretical concept to another, dictating abstract relationships which they *should* understand and then expecting them to make sensible deductions from them, working from formulae — these simply reinforce the students inability to move away from the concrete stage. A few experiences of successful formal thinking, however costly they may appear in time, are educationally more defensible than knowing the *Encyclopedia Britannica* by heart.

LANGUAGE AND INTELLECTUAL DEVELOPMENT

The most important tool in formal thinking is language. Basil Bernstein[7] stressed this and claimed to have demonstrated that children reared in working-class homes acquire what he called a restricted code. He found that in such homes the speech was bare of adjectives and lacking in extended sentences. He contrasted the use of monosyllables and repetitions with the elaborate code used in middle-class homes where the sentences were enriched by a variety of words.

The significance of this difference, claims Bernstein, is that the working-class child is handicapped for the rest of his life by his early verbal poverty. A restricted verbal code has greatest significance during adolescence. It prevents the young person from being able to think effectively in abstract terms and consequently prevents him from coping with the type of hypothetico-deductive sequence described by Piaget. At the lowest intellectual level he 'understands' in terms of feeling, at a higher level he interpolates from his visual experience and only at the highest level does he communicate meaningful abstractions. For example, the following terms are used at the three levels to communicate the same phenomenon:

'hot' or 'live' (tactile),

'high voltage' (derived from the image of a meter),

'high potential relative to earth' (abstract).

Only the latter statement communicates the particular concept with precision, but very few people come to form a meaningful and useful understanding of the concept of potential despite being taught science.

EXPECTATION AND INTELLECTUAL DEVELOPMENT

It is not only the past that can limit a student's ability to progress but also the expectation of his teachers and the attitudes of his peers. D. Hargreaves[8] made a study of the effects of streaming on academic performance at the secondary school level. This study compared the attitudes and attainments of boys in A & B streams with those in C & D streams and found that by and large performance was deeply influenced by the group. In A & B groups it was the norm to get high marks, to please the teacher, to strive for success, and to work well and consistently. The boy who did very well was popular with the rest of the group.

In the C & D stream, however, the situation was reversed. The boy who received praise from the teacher was jeered and rejected by the rest of the group, the only striving was in competition to produce the worst marks, and if a boy actually broke the law he became a kind of hero. In most instances, the boys in these streams were constantly under-achieving: they were seen as victims of their circumstance and once labelled C & D material, they rarely moved out of their stream.

Apart from pointing to the inherent dangers of such streaming this work reiterates the motivational effect of success. The more we as teachers fail and reject students the more we are in danger of destroying any urge they may have had to learn.

As far as capacity to learn is concerned, the average adolescent is as well endowed as he will ever be in his lifetime. He will learn at the peak of his capacity so long as he is sufficiently motivated and at this stage he is usually under tremendous pressure from both family and society to achieve more and more paper qualifications. So long as these are passports to social standing and success, the pressure on young people to sit endless and often meaningless examinations is tantamount to mental cruelty. What further education should attempt to do is not merely provide them with yet more pieces of paper, not merely feed more information into human computers but to help young people find themselves, to encourage them to find their niches in society and more than this to accept them as people in their own right.

EMOTIONAL DEVELOPMENT IN ADOLESCENCE

Just before the onset of adolescence, the young person frequently exhibits exuberance which turns to anger only when he is frustrated. He tends to be outward going and pleasure seeking and forms apparently strong attachments to his peers which may quite suddenly collapse. After the onset of puberty, however, he begins to show some marked emotional changes, he tends to become more reflective and introspective and very often shows a very strong attachment for one other person: usually they both belong to the same group. At this stage he will be described as moody, will become easily angered, and just as easily elated. He spends more time alone and often keeps a very detailed diary of his feelings: he may even start writing poetry. If a boy has athletic tendencies these mood fluctuations are not so noticeable, but he prefers to spend most of his time at his favourite sport and may seem to reject and resent parental interest in the subject. In one instance a boy even neglected to tell his parents that he was selected for the schoolboy's national football team, and gave as his reason that they would make a fuss and want to come and watch him. In many of these cases, the adolescent fears that his parents will make him seem childish, he wants emotional independence and will go to great lengths to achieve it. By the age of sixteen most young people have experienced what they believe to be love. In fact so-called love affairs are common and frequent at this age. Indeed, most psychologists see this period as useful in enabling the young person to learn the sort of personality that matches his own. By the end of adolescence, most young people have settled for a partner of the opposite sex or, at least, know the qualities of the partner they would like.

Adolescence then, is an age of emotional awakening. And as we all once knew, it involves pain and ecstacy, self-analysis and social judgement, the agony of self criticism and the delight of new discoveries and over all, the sense that nobody else has ever before lived through like experiences.

We may try to remember what it was like, but time passes. We lived in a different age albeit only a year or so ago, we had a different set of standards and values, other social crises, other eternal causes. And when we look back we forget those experiences which now reflect to our discredit or discomfort: we no longer know.

Yet our responsibility is to sustain young people. If we wish them to be trustworthy we must trust them, if we want them to co-operate we must co-operate with them and if we want to help them we must be concerned about their welfare. Most adolescents are frank rather than rude, courageous rather than irresponsible, concerned for life rather than aggressive. And they are seeking self-fulfilment. To help them in this quest we must care about them.

REFERENCES

1. Rousseau, J. J., *Emile*, Dent, 1911.
2. Tanner, J. M., *Growth at Adolescence*, 2nd Ed. Blackwell Science Publications.
3. Mead, Margaret, *Growing up in New Guinea*, Penguin, London 1930.
4. Mead, Margaret, *Coming of Age in Samoa*, Penguin, London 1928.
5. Beard, R. N., *An Outline of Piaget's Developmental Psychology*, RKP, 1969.
6. Inhelder, B. and Piaget, J., *The Growth of Logical Thinking*, RKP, 1958.
7. Bernstein, B., *A Socio-linguistic Approach to Social Learning*. The Penguin Survey of Social Sciences 1965.
8. Hargreaves, D., *Social Relations in the Secondary School*, Routledge.

Micro-training

Extended opening of a talk

Each member of the group will prepare the opening of the talk he will present in *Unit Eight*. It will begin with the section already practiced and then go on to briefly outline the content of the talk in the following manner:

'The objective of this talk is that you will be able to solve correctly the second-order differential equations on the test card. I shall divide what I have to say into three (or two, or four) parts as follows:

One_____
Two_____
Three_____   _____,'

At the end of each presentation the group should write down four (or three or five) phrases taken from the talk, one from the heading and one from each sub-section. These should be the phrases that the speaker made to stand out from the rest. These should be given to the speaker who should decide whether they coincide with his intentions. If there is any discrepancy the reason why the emphasis was misplaced should be discussed.

Study Session

FACTORS WHICH INFLUENCE LEARNING

3. *The psychology of learning*

LEARNING

In psychological terms, learning takes place when there is a change of behaviour on the part of the learner.

Thus, for example, we learn in infancy that hunger is unpleasant and that eating relieves hunger, that being comfortable is being warm and dry and well-fed and loved, and that crying will relieve at least some, if not all our discomfort. Thus an infant learns to communicate his needs to his mother, and she, for her part reinforces his communicative signal by responding to those needs. As the child gets older, the communicative signals become more sophisticated and more comprehensible and he is able to make his needs understood more clearly. He further learns that if he is rude in his request his mother may not meet his needs, but that saying 'please' and 'thank-you' and being nice are more successful.

So, in these terms, we are in fact born learners and almost every experience we have will, in some way, modify our behaviour.

However, it is not so easy to observe behaviour changes when a teacher stands in front of a class and teaches students a purely theoretical subject. In such cases we can measure the learning effectiveness by means of questions and tests and the change in behaviour becomes manifest in the manner in which the test is answered.

Learning implies that we have come to know what was previously unknown, and this knowing involves knowing *how* and knowing *that*. Knowing *how* refers to the achievement of skills which include social skills, language skills and general motor skills. Knowing *that* refers to the acquisition of knowledge and the understanding of subject matter. Knowing *how* and knowing *that* both mould our behaviour to some lesser or greater degree.

Insofar as this moulding or changing of another's behaviour is fundamental to the teaching/learning process, it follows that by examining the mental mechanisms which bring about the change we can, perhaps, enhance the efficacy of the process.

Now, since most human behaviour is the physical or mental expression of learned responses, learning is a proper study for psychologists. As with any other discipline special terms are used to describe and explain learning processes and at times there is a danger of becoming positively bewitched by the stylistic terminology which has grown around learning theories.

What we have to bear in mind, however, is that any specialized linguistic pattern whether it is technical or colloquial is merely the user's hat-stand on which he hangs ideas. And so it is with the psychology of learning: it puts into rather special words explanations and theories, some of which you and I may have claimed to know all along, but have been unable to express because of the restrictions of everyday speech. But more than just presenting us with verbal tools for expression, the psychology of learning provides us with a scientific background of knowledge which ought to direct our teaching along more positive and constructive lines.

The difficulty of accepting that psychology is a science is the temptation to look for the kinds of laws we find in physical science. If, for instance, we can say that A causes B and then prove that it does, we feel better about it. The fact that this frequently cannot be done in the psychology of learning is borne out by the numerous and often seemingly conflicting theories which have arisen in this area. Learning, of course, is a very complicated process occurring in many forms and situations and it is therefore necessary to recognize that learning theory as it stands today, is a somewhat inelegant and unfinished product of a continuing study. Nevertheless, in saying this, we also know that there are some fairly fundamental and stable principles which serve to tell us not only what learning is like but also what it is not like.

Different schools of psychology and different investigators have used different models to study and the greatest difference is the situational one, so that we may say that an individual learns in *this* fashion when confronted by *this* particular situation: no more and no less. For sometimes the models resemble the learning of a school child or a college student and sometimes they seem better to resemble the learning of a chimpanzee or a rat or a pigeon.

Strategic planning of teaching or instruction should start with a clear and precise statement of objectives — behavioural if possible — desired at the end of the period of instruction; this instruction can then be arranged with a view to bringing about the kind of change we hope for.

Insofar as educational objectives so often mean different things to different people, it is important to be as precise as possible. Perhaps the most valuable guide in this field is Bloom's *Taxonomy*[1] and the reader is urged, at this stage, to acquaint himself with this work.

Having established the objective in behavioural terms we then have the task of selecting the means for achieving the desired end. This calls for a consideration of learning theory. Basic to a consideration of learning theory is the simple statement that the fundamental aim of teaching is the promotion of learning, and that students learn when they want to learn, when they know how to learn and when they are able to learn. And of these, wanting to learn, or motivation, underlies the whole study of method.

MOTIVATION

Little children are obviously motivated by curiosity — they seem naturally to want to know things. Older students however, often seem to have wearied of learning and need more than mere opportunity or the promise of future reward. They need their inner minds to tell them that this is living *now* and worthwhile *now*.

We have previously discussed in Unit One, the six major sources of motivation to work and now we should take a closer look at the additional motivational influences that affect an individual's performance in the classroom. Motivation, as a term, is a generic one commonly used to describe some sort of stimulus which activates goal-directed behaviour. Much that has been written on the subject of motivation concentrates on the maintenance of constant physical and chemical conditions within the body irrespective of external change — the so-called homeostatic principle. We are motivated by our body chemistry and such drives are essential for our survival.

But the term motivation is much wider than this, it embraces the source of internal energy which sustains certain patterns of behaviour. We must concern ourselves with the ways in which motivation affects a person's ability to learn, and how we can help to motivate students to learn more effectively. Many studies have been carried out to attempt to classify the nature of learning motivation. McClelland[2] and others made a study of American Indians and attempted to find out why some children seemed to need to excel whilst others were content to plod along in a mediocre way. They found that the high achievers came from homes in which they were taught early independence and were expected to cope with situations for which other children were considered too young. These children then, were reared to depend less on their parents than were their peers, and they constantly achieved higher grades. Those from the more protective homes seemed content to achieve mediocre grades.

This was followed by many further studies in which sophisticated tests were devised to discover what environmental factors were significant in performance rates. The social class factor created much attention and works by J. W. B. Douglas,[3] E. E. Fraser[4] and J. E. Floud,[5] make it clear that the child who does best at school is more likely to come from a middle-class home than not. Later work attempted to classify the factors within the home which contributed to this superior performance. One which constantly emerged was that poor performance at school correlates with at least some domestic difficulties such as poor housing, financial hardship, parental attitudes to education and so on.

J. McVeigh Hunt[6] showed how we can use intrinsic motivation to teach young children. His scheme is one in which we constantly put to the child a logical sequence of problems each progressively more complicated than its predecessor. When the child has coped with one stage, the next stage is presented to him. He maintains that a learning stage is intrinsically motivating if it is just a little more complex than the previous one and by carefully structuring what is to be learned, a teacher can design for each child programmes designed to encourage him to achieve at a higher level. These four additional bases of motivation which relate particularly to learning can be summarized as follows:

1. Achievement motivation — knowing from other previous experiences that you can be equally or more successful than your colleagues.

2. Home environment — the level of achievement does not merely depend upon a student's social class origin, but also upon the extent to which his parents have encouraged and taken an interest in his performance.

3. Aspiration — reflects parental attitudes and interest in a student's education.

4. Difficulty itself is a motivator provided the student anticipates success.

OTHER FACTORS

Students learn when they know how to learn. This is particularly important to older students who have returned to studies after a break. Their first few days should involve them in learning how and when to take notes, how to use the library, what to read, how to ask questions and how to assess their own progress.

Finally, students learn when they are able to learn, that is when *they* have the mental capacity to learn and when *we* have been successful in arranging the subject matter in such a way that it is comprehensible to them.

The ability to learn is basically a function of a student's intelligence. We need not concern ourselves at this stage whether intelligence is a consequence of nature or nurture or even Guinness and oysters — the fact is that some students think and react as though they are endowed with highly efficient brains whilst others do not and we must acknowledge these differences. To treat a student with the intelligence of an average 10 year old child to the teaching pressures that are appropriate to one with that of a 16 year old is as cruel as demanding the same physical work from a child as from a coal miner: indeed the effect may be even more cruel in terms of future mental anguish.

Difficulty is not a deterrent to learning — hopelessness is the end of intellectual willpower. So we should regulate our demands to suit the intelligence of our students. We should not be surprised if sixteen year olds are unable to discriminate between 'dividing by' and 'dividing into' and we should, equally, not be surprised if sixteen year olds are able to discuss electromagnetic radiation with understanding. But we should look for signposts which lie beneath what students say and do and be guided to accommodate our demands to their capacities.

LEARNING PROCESSES

The main prototypes of learning theory are usually classified as follows:
1. *Associationism* — learning an unknown topic because it reminds us of one we already know.
2. *Conditioning* — learning to perform a task to a signal.
3. *Rote learning* — learning to memorize parts or lists or tables.
4. *Insight learning* — learning to gain understanding and to structure concepts.
5. *Motor skill learning* — learning to acquire manual dexterity.

ASSOCIATIONISM

This was probably the earliest of learning theories and is attributed to Aristotle. He claimed that we learned and remembered things because we were able to associate new knowledge with previously learned material. He said that A may remind us of B for one of three reasons:
(a) because A and B are similar
(b) because they are contrasting
(c) because they are contiguous, that is they are always seen or heard etc., together.
In teaching physical exercises to music, association is used to provide a cue to what is to be learned and then the cue is gradually withdrawn. For example — 'Press, press, press — stretch,

good, good. Press, press' . . . etc. If this is accompanied by clapping and music, the first new association link could be the clapping when the desired response will be made to — Clap, clap, clap . . . Clap, clap, clap with an occasional 'good' thrown in and finally the clapping can stop and the learner performs the exercises to the music alone.

In teaching the solution of simple equations:

$$2x + 7 = 15$$

might be written on the board. Then after an explanation the words — 'Subtract 7 from both sides of the equation', might be said and at the same time the 7 and 15 tapped with a pointer. This, repeated IN EXACTLY THE SAME WAY a number of times would lead to the stage when a student who hesitates when asked what to do in this case:

$$6x + 3 = 21$$

would give the correct response once the 3 and the 21 were tapped EXACTLY AS BEFORE. The correct response should then be rewarded by a smile or a word of praise.

Learning when to apply the law of moments can be taught by saying the words 'Golden rule' or touching a metre rule whenever the law should be recalled. Again, the correct response leads to a 'reward'.

In every such case, a cue is associated with the required response and is used to provide the student with sufficient confidence in his mastery over the procedure to enable him to further develop his insight into why the procedure is valid.

BUT, if this mode of teaching is to be truly effective the teacher must KNOW WHAT HE IS DOING or the students may be confused and frustrated by a variety of similar stimuli, by hesitancy on the part of the teacher, by being uncertain of their success because of the apparent absence of a 'reward'. The 'reward' may well be a mixture of the teacher's praise of acceptance of the standard produced or it may be an endogenous reinforcement, that is a feeling of self-satisfaction at the successful completion of a task, but here the student must know he *has* been successful.

There is, of course a danger in making associations to the exclusion of understanding. We have all felt this neurosis when suddenly faced with a choice and having no guidelines for a decision. The P.E. to music performers described earlier would feel this if the waltz-time suddenly changed to say, tango-time: the simple equation student, if he had no insight into the process might gabble incoherently if $2x + 7y = 0$ were put on the board and the $7y$ and 0 were tapped. And presented for the first time with forces on a lamina instead of forces on a rod, the same response could well result from the teacher touching a metre rule.

TOLMAN'S FIELD COGNITION THEORY

This rudimentary theory of associationism has now become included in more sophisticated ones such as Tolman's Field-Cognition theory. Tolman argued that learning depends on the building up of what he calls 'cognitive maps' from learning experiences. New problems are referred to these cognitive maps which indicate the key to their solution. The more inter-related the learning experiences which are gained the more comprehensive the cognitive maps become, and the more comprehensive the maps then the greater the chance that transfer of learning will take place.

In attempting to find a solution to a problem we commonly start with a familiar routine. If that fails we try others and each routine builds up a series of hypotheses which is linked with the preceding set until the problem is solved. Having solved the problem the mediating processes are stored in a mental bank and called upon in future problems.

For example, when we are first shown how to get from one place to another, we store certain 'signposts' in our mind. 'Walk to the traffic island with a telegraph post on it . . . go down the road with a garage on one corner . . . turn left at the letter box' . . . and so on. Each time we 'solve the problem' of making this journey our mental map of the route becomes more complete. To find a new route we constantly refer to the old until the new one is established. Notice that we must know where we want to go — we must have a clear idea of our objective — and we must have some understanding of the route before we start albeit an incomplete one. We must also have previously learned certain skills and knowledge: how to walk, how to avoid being run over being obvious ones.

Similarly, to draw an electric bell circuit we begin by drawing the electromagnet, perhaps; then the armature because that is what the magnet moves, then the contact-breaker because the hammer must move to and fro and finally the wires and the rest. Each time we draw the diagram we generate a more complete mental image of it until the sequence of drawing loses its importance.

When we solve a quadratic equation we first learn the signposts: collect together all the terms in x^2, in x and the numbers. Arrange them in order to the left of the equation. Factorize and so on. When the problem becomes too complex to fit this procedure, separate steps are modified and a new map produced for these more complicated problems. We can allow ourselves the luxury of fully understanding 'why' when we have the security of knowing 'how'.

In teaching we should therefore emphasize the signposts from which the earliest cognitive maps will be constructed. Critical steps should be made to stand out clearly against the material that supports them and the sequence of these critical steps should be emphasized and recapitulated. No students should believe a detail to be of critical consequence because it occupied too much of his interest or attention or because the teacher over-emphasized it. Even if he understands nothing of the subject matter, an intelligent observer should be able to follow the form of the 'cognitive map' when a new area of subject is being taught. That is one of the reasons for having teachers instead of books. This theory underlies the micro-training exercise at the end of the previous section.

CLASSICAL CONDITIONING

This is the name given to a specific training procedure developed by Ivan-Pavlov, a Russian Psychologist, at the beginning of the century. Pavlov in fact started his work by studying the digestive system of dogs and in particular the salivary processes and their function in relation to digestion. He then went on to develop his classical conditioning theory. He found that the dog not only salivated when food was placed in front of it but also salivated at the approaching sounds associated with the placement of the food. Pavlov went on to show that if a bell was rung at the same time as the food arrived, the bell could become the *conditional stimulus* and the act of salivation that occurred when the bell rang would become the *conditional response.* He demonstrated this by getting the dog fully accustomed to the sound of the bell when it was feeding time, after which the dog would salivate at the sound of a bell only. The dog went on salivating at the sound of the bell so long as the food arrived after it, but when it was not re-inforced by the reward of food the salivation at the sound of the bell ceased — there was extinction of the conditional response.

Classical conditioning shows as involuntary emotional responses, which it is felt by many workers have arisen through an unconditional stimulus. Pavlov demonstrated a form of neurosis in a dog which he had conditioned to salivate at a circle and not at an ellipse. Gradually he reduced the difference in shape between the two figures until the dog was unable to discriminate between them. The dog was faced with a conflict, not knowing which figure to salivate at and as a result, the poor beast was reduced to a neurotic outburst of squealing, barking and violence.

We are, of course, conditioned in many ways. Our attitudes to controversial issues are to some extent influenced in this way by the mass media and one relevant example of this is the attitude many people have towards students. During the 1960s the television and press gave much space and time 'exposing' student behaviour, notably in the numerous demonstrations that were taking place at the time. Students were shown in peaceful demonstrations, in less peaceful demonstrations, in sit-ins, protests and so on. Gradually, students found it difficult to get accommodation and to get part-time jobs and increasingly older people had come to believe that all students were rebellious, untidy, dirty and work-shy. This attitude exists in many people today and we should be particularly concerned to establish positive and helpful attitudes based upon actual experience rather than on conditioning from whatever source.

OPERANT OR INSTRUMENTAL CONDITIONING

This is a theory of learning which some people attribute, in the first place to the work of E. L. Thorndike (1911) and what he called the 'law of effect'. But B. F. Skinner (1938) developed the basic idea and as a result produced his theory of operant conditioning. Basically, the theory centres around the notion that behaviour depends upon reinforcement which may be positive or negative. Thus a behaviour pattern will be repeated if the rewards give satisfaction but deterred if its effect is punishing. Skinner's analysis of instruction assumes that there is already motivation, that the student will make a response and that for learning to occur this response should be rewarded or re-inforced. Whilst some later work on the subject claims that frequency of the reward or punishment weakens the response, other workers claim that reward powerfully strengthens the stimulus-response sequence and is a most significant factor in all human learning. Punishment, on the other hand, may be of bene-fit initially but usually does ultimate harm by causing rebellion or antipathy to the learning. Skinner's work leads to some rela-tively specific suggestions about the design of instruction. He talks about *stimulus control* in which he suggests ways of manipulating the stimulus so that it becomes more forceful to the learner so as to bring about more precise and elaborate behaviour changes or learning patterns. He also talks of *shaping of behaviour* by means of carefully structuring a sequence of re-inforcements in order to bring about distinct patterns of motor acts. Skinner suggests that the sequence of reinforcement should be so devised that at each separate stage of learning the desired response is reinforced. This is particularly relevant to the performance of motor acts involving practice and repetition at each stage.

Skinner also talks about *chaining*, in which a more complex learning structure is achieved by arranging the conditions of re-inforcement in a step-by-step procedure, each step being linked with the one before so as to ensure that the final step is always connected with the others which precede it. Skinner's theories led to the development of linear programmed learning techniques (see Unit 15).

In the field of social psychology, Robert Rosenthal and Lenore Jacobson[7] investigated the effect of 'cues' given by the teacher and based on his expectancy of the pupil's performance. What they found was, not only that pupils tended to behave in the way the teacher expected them to behave but that the teacher reinforced various behaviour patterns by means of 'cues', which seemed, for the most part, involuntary. In particular, they weighed the effect of a smile, for when a teacher was given a response which was consistent with his expectations, he would nod his approval, smile and look altogether more pleasant. This is probably the teacher's most powerful reinforcer. Similarly, they found that when teachers were informed that a group was less bright, their expectancy was lower and they taught less to the group who consequently learned less. In other words, the nature of reinforcement looks somewhat circular in that it has a self-fulfilling character, and what we have to be careful of is not how we reinforce the students behaviour, because with practice that can be controlled, but the extent to which we ourselves are being reinforced by the students' behaviour and by our expectancy of their ability to learn.

Another theorist whose findings have a direct application to what we do in the college, is Gagné.[8] He classified seven major kinds of mental processes which are called learning. Each is different from the others and each calls for a different set of learning conditions. They are:

1. *Signal learning* — classical conditioning.
2. *Stimulus-response learning* — learning by associations or operant conditioning.
3. *Motor and verbal chain learning* — learning skill sequences or language.
4. *Multiple discrimination* — distinguishing between similar words, for instance.
5. *Concept learning* — able to make a common response to a class of stimuli that may differ widely from one another.

6. *Principle learning* — connecting and arranging concepts.
7. *Problem solving* — thinking. Combining two or more principles to produce a new capability that can be shown to depend on a 'higher order' principle.

He considers that the typical learning of young people in further and higher education may involve all of these types of learning but that some are much more frequent than others in particular subject areas. Thus certain motor and verbal chain learning may be necessary when learning a new foreign language but this type of learning would probably never be met in courses in history, government or English composition. Many of the so-called theoretical subjects taught at advanced or technical college level involve the kinds of learning that Gagné described as concept learning, principle learning and problem solving. He goes on to say that all types of learning may require certain general conditions to be effective and these would include some rote learning, some reinforcement and so on. But there are specific conditions necessary for each level of learning and coming to terms with principles or the solving of a problem demands a different set of conditions from those required in learning a new concept like electromotive force or virus and so on.

Gagné's second principle is what he calls 'cumulative learning'. The basis of this is that new learning depends on the kind of learning that has gone on before, and learning is therefore seen as a gradual building up process of knowledge. It stresses that it is not enough for the student to have 'had' previous instruction of a subject or topic before proceeding further, he must have 'mastered' the topic and know it thoroughly in the way it should be known before he can cope with the next stage. In all instances, there are specific prerequisite learnings before the new learning task can be undertaken and these form a hierarchy. Before it is possible to understand a principle at the top of the hierarchy it is necessary to act in accordance with all the principles below it; there is, in other words, a *structure* of knowledge. As an example, consider the learning of the principle of flotation. This can be learned only after principles and concepts below it in the table have already been learned.

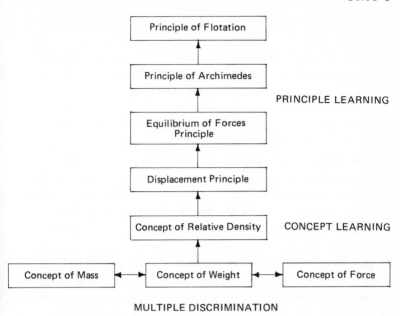

This level of learning corresponds to Piaget's level of formal reasoning[9] which, he holds, is beyond the intellectual group of children under the age of eleven and cannot be fully achieved until the age of sixteen. In some accounts, he calls the mental process involved, the hypothetico-deductive sequence of thought.

Both general observation and experience seem to show that many students in further education — perhaps half of them — never reach this stage either because they are not called upon to exercise the thinking processes that it demands or because they have not mastered and maintained their mastery over the earlier learning processes which this level demands or because they are intellectually unable to think at this level.

GESTALT THEORIES

The Gestalt theories originated from a German school of psychology founded by Köhler, Wertheimer and Koffka. They felt that learning was not merely a series of S-R (stimulus-response) steps, but that there was a much more complex process of internalization which goes on in problem-solving situations.

Köhler claimed to have demonstrated as much with a chimpanzee whom he observed learning to join sticks together in order to obtain a banana which was otherwise out of reach. Köhler claimed that insight or understanding of the whole problem requires the ability and opportunity to literally sit down and think of all its aspects which might lead to a solution. He claimed that learning takes place when an individual is able to internalize a problem into a whole conceptual structure; there needs to be insight into the whole problem before it can be solved. If we attempt to use behavioural terms to explain this we can say that the stimulus is the presence of the problem, the response is the solution of the problem and the mental mechanism which brings about the solution we can call the 'mediating process'.

Some later theorists have complained of its oversimplicity. Hull,[10] for example, believed that insight learning was composed of stimulus producing responses insofar as each sequential response formed the stimulus for futher responses, and that the mediating process in a complex problem solving situation is merely anticipatory in its nature. This is clearly linked with the work of Galperin who stressed the importance of what he called the anticipatory schemata — the thinking process by which the individual is able to anticipate the solution to the next step. For Galperin,[11] this is particularly relevant in the teaching of science. He found that where groups of pupils were conducting experiments, the observing pupils were often able to anticipate the outcome of an experiment more readily than the pupils who were actually carrying it out. He concluded that practical activity tends to hamper creative conceptualization and that practical work should be used for refining rather than learning. Learning from demonstration, he says is most effective if the sequence of doing and telling is so designed that the learner verbally anticipates the steps the demonstrator is going to take.

For Ausubel,[12] school and college learning is meaningful learning and is quite different from the process that is generally called rote learning. He cites four very important principles basic to the psychology of learning and based on the notion of insight.

The first of these principles is what he calls 'subsumption'. Meaningful learning takes place when a new idea is subsumed into (or soaked into) a related structure of already existing knowledge, resulting in the acquisition of a set of new meanings. It consists of providing the learner with a meaningful structure before he undertakes the learning of a new principle and this constitutes an 'organizer' which bears a logical overview for what is to be learned. To somewhat oversimplify this: rather than requiring students to learn the characteristics of, say, 'squamous epithelium and ciliated epithelium' they would be told before hand that they were going to study 'the different types of tissue in the body'. This would constitute the organizer.

The second principle of Ausubel is called 'progressive differentiation' and relates to the content of what is learned: it consists of dealing with very general and inclusive ideas first, and then proceeding to the more specific and detailed ones later.

His third principle is called 'consolidation' and like Gagné, he insists that there must be mastery of each stage before proceeding to more advanced stages.

The last principle in this theory is termed 'integrative reconciliation'. By this, Ausubel means that all new ideas must be seen to have some logical association with previous learning, and where these are not obvious, the learner must be made aware of the similarities and the differences so that there will be a reconciliation of any real or apparent inconsistencies.

Ausubel's theory adds up to a pretty strong specification of how instructional material should be organized and presented for most effective learning, for it tells us what to do first, what sequence should follow, what to do to ensure remembering and what outcome to expect.

SUMMARY

We learn when we *want* to learn. Motivation to learn may come from our bodily needs — drives — from social and group pressures, from anticipation of success.

We learn when we are able to learn and know how to learn. Learning theories are broadly classified as Associationism, conditioning, rote-learning, insight learning and motor skill learning.

Learning progresses through a hierarchy from signal learning to problem solving and each level calls for different learning conditions.

REFERENCES

1. Bloom, B. S., *Taxonomy of Educational Objectives Handbook I and II*, Longman, London 1965.
2. McClelland, D. C., Atkinson, J. W., Clark, R. A. and Lowell, E. L., *The Achievement Motive*, Appleton–Century–Crofts, 1953.
3. Douglas, J. W. B., *Home and the School*, MacGibbon & Kee, London 1964.
4. Fraser, Elizabeth, *Home Environment and the School*, University of London Press 1959.
5. Floud, J., *Social Class and Educational Opportunity*, Heinemann, 1956.
6. McVeigh Hunt, J., *Educational Technology*, 11, 1971.
7. Rosenthal, R., and Jacobson, L., *Pygmalion in the classroom: teacher expectation and pupils' intellectual development*, Holt, Rinehart & Winston, New York 1968.
8. Gagné, R. M., *The Conditions of Learning*, Holt, Rinehart & Winston, New York 1965.
9. Inhelder, B. and Piaget, J., *The Growth of Logical Thinking: From Childhood to Adolescence*, Basic Books, 1958.
10. Hull, C. L., *Principles of Behaviour*, Appleton, 1943.
11. Brian Simon, Ed., *Psychology in the Soviet Union*, Routledge, Kegan, Paul, London 1957.
12. Ausubel, D. P., *The Psychology of Meaningful Verbal Learning*, Grune and Stratton, 1963.
13. Hebb, D. O., 'Drives and the CNS (Conceptual Nervous System)', *Psychological Review*, 62, 1955.

Practical Exercise

Learning exercises

1. The group leader will teach a member of the group to repeat accurately a set of numbers.

   The subject will sit in front of the group. Each group member and the leader will have copies of the table on p. 90. The leader will read the numbers at a regular pace and with no emphases: he will read them a second time. The subject will now attempt to say the numbers and immediately after he says the first one the leader will say it correctly, similarly with the second, third and so on to the eighth. If the subject cannot remember he will say any number knowing that the leader will say the correct one immediately afterwards. Each time the subject is correct the group members will mark a cross in the corresponding space in the first row of the spaces. The procedure will be repeated over and over again until the subject has learned the correct sequence. The group will now discuss the following:

(*a*) Why did the learning pattern turn out as it did?

(*b*) What effect did stress have on the learner's performance?

(*c*) How did the learner try to remember the sequence?

In this discussion refer back to any learning theories that seem relevant.

2. The exercise on p. 91 is a code in which numbers are represented by letters.

The code is a logical system, try to solve it.

Discuss the mental processes that occurred during the exercise — in particular:

(*a*) Why did you not give up sooner?

(*b*) How did you go about solving the problem?

In the discussion, refer back to any learning theories that seem relevant.

LEARNING EXERCISE 1

34	19	28	52	71	85	53	92
34	19	28	52	71	85	53	92

LEARNING EXERCISE 2

Number	Symbol	Number	Symbol	Number	Symbol
0	x	16	dq	49	cdc
1	c	17	dp	71	cpp
2	d	18	tx	72	dxx
3	t	19	tc	108	txx
4	q	20	td	109	txc
5	p	24	qx	110	txd
6	cx	27	qt	111	txt
7	cc	30	px	145	qxc
8	cd	35	pp	180	pxx
9	ct	36	cxx	200	ptd
10	cq	37	cxc	215	ppp
11	cp	38	cxd	216	cxxx
12	dx	41	cxp	220	cxxq
13	dc	42	ccx	432	dxxx
14	dd	48	cdx	468	dcxx
15	dt			500	dcpd

Micro-training

Use of chalkboard or flip-chart

1. Each group member to state the opening of the talk to be given in *Unit Eight*. He will then write the heading on a board or chart and underline it. He will then repeat the heading.
2. Each group member will make a diagram on the board or chart of the shape of his living-room and the main items of furniture in it, and label them. As he does so he will describe the room and its contents.

   By using colour he will make one particular item stand out as though it is to be the major subject of a talk.

   The group will discuss the effectiveness of the different colours and techniques used in this exercise.

Unit 7

Exercise

Preparation of a talk

The talk to be given in *Unit Eight* should now be prepared. It should be designed to cause learning to take place, should last for 15 minutes and should not include any feedback from the group.

The preparation should include:

1. The objective of the talk given in behavioural terms (Unit Two).
2. The objective test for assessing the success of the talk (Unit Three).
3. Use of the chalkboard or flip-chart (Unit Six).
4. The main headings of the sections of the talk (Unit Six).
5. Any other notes that seem necessary.

The extended opening of the talk (Unit Six) and the closing of the talk (Unit Two) should be given without reference to notes in order fully to exploit non verbal signals.

Notes are best restricted to main headings.

Unit 8

Practical Exercise
Giving a talk

Each group member to present the talk prepared in *Unit Seven*. At the end of each talk the group will complete the test and mark it.

The marks will be written on the board by the member who has presented the talk and converted to a block diagram showing their distribution — thus:

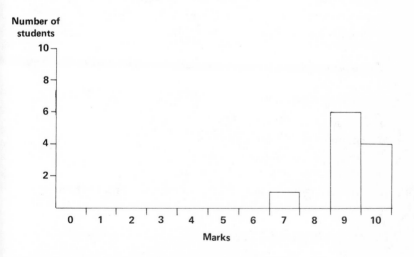

The significance of the result should be discussed.

After each talk, group members will fill in the following rating scales and prepare a rating profile for each speaker.

Rating Scales for Short Talks

Guide

KNOWLEDGE OF SUBJECT AND PREPARATION OF TALK

A. Knowledge

1. Clearly inadequate.
2. I felt I could not rely on him.
3. He seemed to know enough for the talk and that is all.
4. He seemed to know more than was needed.
5. He is clearly an authority.

```
1          2          3          4          5
```

B. Choice of appropriate illustrations or examples — verbal or pictorial

1. These enhanced the talk and clarified its message.
2. These were apt and interesting as well as useful.
3. These were useful.
4. They interfered with the sequence and/or called for as much mental effort as that which they illustrated.
5. No attempt to illustrate where illustration was essential.

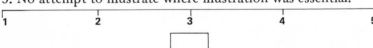
```
1          2          3          4          5
```

C. Organization of talk

1. The sequence was muddled.
2. The plan was badly sequenced.
3. The sequence was reasonable.
4. The arrangement added interest.
5. The arrangement added interst and aided understanding.

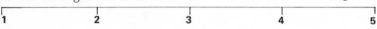
```
1          2          3          4          5
```

PERSONAL QUALITIES

D. Voice

1. Unpleasant to hear and distracting.
2. Unpleasant.

3. It neither aided nor detracted from the comprehensibility of the talk but was not unpleasant.
4. Interesting to listen to.
5. Used as an instrument to motivate and enhance understanding.

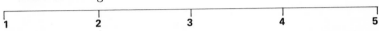

E. Command of Language _____

F. Non-verbal Signals

1. Inappropriate and distracting.
2. Noticeably unsuitable.
3. Not evident.
4. Emphasize the verbal messages.
5. Motivate and emphasize the verbal messages.

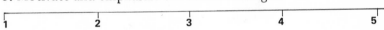

PERFORMANCE

G. Mode of Communication

1. Overbearingly authoritative.
3. Inclined to be 'bossy'.
5. Collaborative and showed evident interest in responses.
3. Used personality rather than reason to persuade.
1. Relied upon good nature of group to continue — lacked drive.

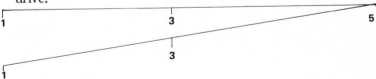

H. Maintenance of Interest

1. Totally absorbing.
2. Very interesting

3. Held my attention.
4. My attention wandered from time to time.
5. Boring.

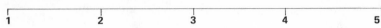

Rating Scales for short talks

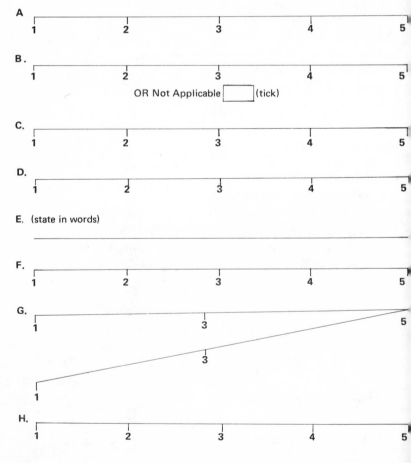

A
1   2   3   4   5

B.
1   2   3   4   5

OR Not Applicable [   ] (tick)

C.
1   2   3   4   5

D.
1   2   3   4   5

E. (state in words)
_____

F.
1   2   3   4   5

G.
1   3   5
3
1

H.
1   2   3   4   5

PROFILE

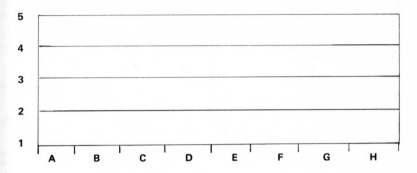

Module III

Teaching students

Unit 9

Study Session

The analysis of a lesson

Much of our teaching life takes place in a classroom and our teaching commonly takes the form of lessons. In recent years it has become fashionable to develop new methods of teaching and at times, the lesson has tended to fall into some disrepute. We believe that the lesson is far from obsolete, and we are not alone in our belief. In *The Process of Schooling* by J. M. Stephens (Holt, Rinehard and Winston) 1967 . . . the conclusion drawn from comparative studies of teaching methods was that as long as the teacher has a strong interest in his subject and is able to communicate this interest, what he does is relatively unimportant. Now a strong interest in a subject is, in itself, a motivational pressure to teach and to prepare in advance, and in general it shows as active teaching — as lessons — as experiences the teacher shares with his students. Less sweeping, perhaps were the findings from a study conducted with some 280 secondary school children in Edinburgh. The object of the study was to see which method of teaching would prove most effective in changing the children's attitude and it was hoped, their behaviour in regard to cigarette smoking. Four methods of teaching were used; the didactic approach, group discussion, psychological persuasion and total project. Of these there was only significant change in behaviour when the didactic or lesson approach was used. (L. M. Watson, *Cigarette smoking in school children*, Edinburgh Health Bulletin 24, 1966.)

Since we believe that the lesson will survive the onslaught of the more dilettante and esoteric theorists, we aim to spend some time looking at how best we can use the lesson and how the best lessons are used. When we employ value judgements like these to describe a teaching performance we should qualify our meaning of 'best lessons'. This is difficult, but when observing student teachers on teaching practice, or training officers at work, or watching our colleagues give lessons, we have seen some really stirling performances, lessons which hold the students' interest from the very first word, and sparkle along to the enjoyment and learning efficiency of all. And from time to time, all of us have shared this experience, we do not need anyone to tell us that it was a 'good' lesson; from the experience itself and the effects it achieves we know, just as we know on those other occasions when a lesson falls flat. But when we come to look at and attempt to analyse these best lessons, we can do no more than lay down a framework around which a competent teacher can create his really good lessons. We are *not* saying that every lesson must have this or that form, or that every lesson plan must conform to the one we suggest. For we believe that teaching is largely an art and the good teacher creates his art in the classroom. If it is not seen in this light, it becomes toil and the years bring disillusionment and the students suffer.

Our terms of reference then, are these: a lesson is a teaching session, so planned that at each stage of its development the method used is the one most likely to promote efficient learning in that particular situation. It involves the participation of students and may embarrass shy learners. It is eminently suitable for groups of about twenty. It calls for a high degree of ability on the part of the teacher who must accept the responsibility for motivating the students and for causing them to learn, and he does this by selecting and adapting methods of teaching, by organizing his material and by behaving in a way that will make them *want* to learn. For in a large measure, students learn by reason of the thoroughness of the teacher's preparation and by preparation, we mean everything we can arrange to make teaching more effective.

THE ORGANIZATIONAL BACKGROUND

In most of our teaching we have at least to attempt to cover a syllabus; that is, the list of subject matter that the students are expected to learn about. We say 'attempt' because when we come to examine some syllabuses the task that is presented seems quite unreasonable, and yet a serious attempt has to be made.

As a first step, the syllabus should be re-organized into a scheme of work — that is an ordered sequence of subject matter, arranged in such a way as to suit the age and abilities of the students. It should, in general, begin with the easiest-to-learn subject matter and go on to the more difficult but it must, of course, seem reasonable to the students; for example, although it is easy to understand how an electric relay works it would be pointless to teach about it before, say, the three effects of an electric current. Furthermore, the scheme should begin with lessons designed to give a general overview of the whole course of study.

Finally, the scheme should, wherever possible, fit in or correlate with other schemes of work which they will follow and this calls for consultation with other members of staff. The resulting scheme of work should then be broken down into lessons.

As each lesson is taught it should be recorded very very briefly so that the teacher — or more especially his substitute if the teacher should be absent — can know what the class has already studied. A record should also be kept of the attendances and attainments of the students and these should include notes about their interest and persistence as well as their marks.

Before starting a lesson then, we need the following:

1. A copy of the syllabus.
2. A copy of the scheme of work.
3. The record of work covered by the students to date.
4. Individual records of attainments and attendances of students.
5. A lesson plan.
6. Aids.
7. Reference material (Fig. 12).

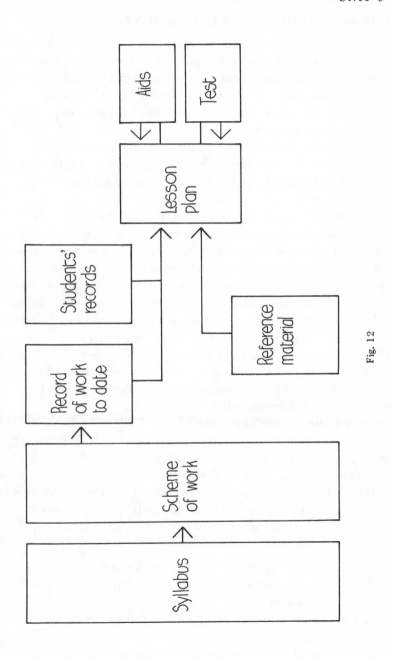

Fig. 12

THE SOCIOLOGICAL BACKGROUND

Teaching is an affair of social relationships and learning derives
from social interactions. It is important that within the classroom we establish successful learning as normal so that students
anticipate success, and we can achieve this by making success
seem attainable and desirable. To this end we *must* aim to create
a healthy learning climate, one that is harmonious rather than
stressful. We must recognize too the need our students feel to
work as a group rather than as isolated individuals and this will
be promoted through discussion and syndicate methods,
through group projects and so on.

Whatever else we may like to believe about the teacher, whilst
he is teaching he is psychologically superior to his students. And
what is more, students prefer it that way. They feel more comfortable when they know that the teacher can teach them something new, and when they know the teacher is an expert in his
subject. The teacher, then, is likely to be more successful in his
role when the students see him as a creditable source of information. It is crucial here for the teacher to fix his sights accurately.
If the students feel him to be intellectually overbearing he loses
the vital rapport essential to good relationships with his class; if
on the other hand he over-simplifies the students will feel be-
littled and their learning efficiency will fall.

Indeed, the teacher's best way of redressing this psychological
imbalance of superiority when he needs to do so is by being very
much himself, by enjoying fun, by showing enthusiasm for his
subject and delight at his students' successes.

Having turned these questions over in our minds we can look
more closely at the practical issues that affect performance.

There are three focal points of any teaching situation and
these are:

1. The student . . . his needs, his goals, his aspirations.
2. The subject matter . . . the scope and depth to which it
should be learned.
3. The teacher and his potential for making learning
worthwhile.

In a lesson all three must be woven together to produce an

experience which is both valuable and enjoyable, and as an outcome . . . LEARNING MUST TAKE PLACE.

To ensure that it does, it is useful to pose and answer the following questions:

1. *What am I going to teach?*
   Here, we try to see what we are going to do in relation to what has gone on before and this involves some consideration of the syllabus, some consideration of the scheme of work and some reflection on recent developments that have occurred in the subject.

2. *Who am I going to teach?*
   It is of prime importance to consider the students' social and academic backgrounds, their linguistic codes, their capabilities, general knowledge and experience.

3. *Why am I going to teach this topic?*
   In the first place, we must be able to state behavioural objectives, that is the behaviour changes we hope to bring about through this particular learning experience. We ask if the topic has relevance to the students' goals and whether it is necessary for the understanding of subsequent matter. We consider OUR aims in presenting this topic and ask if they match with the students' aims in learning it.

4. *Where am I going to teach this subject?*
   We consider what facilities will be available; whether, for example, it is a noisy room, and whether the environment will distract or stimulate the students. We check small details; is there a chalkboard, duster and chalk; is there a clock?

5. *When am I going to teach this subject?*
   Here we ask what the students will have been doing prior to the period. The time of day at which a lesson happens is important. First period they may be sleepy, second period is usually lively, first period after lunch may depend on the physical quality of the lunch and so on. In general there is much to be said for teaching theoretical subjects in the morning and practical ones in the afternoon.

6. *How am I going to teach this subject?*
   This is, perhaps, the most crucial question. We have to arrive

at a decision as to which is the best method or methods to use in this particular teaching situation with this particular group. We consider the teaching aids that are available and the kind of learning we want to take place.

Having considered these questions we now prepare the lesson.

STRUCTURE OF A LESSON

1. Introduction

This should include a statement of intent which if at all possible, should take the form of a behavioural objective. It should generally be preceded by some revision of previous work. Thus, the opening may consolidate the previous lesson, by question and answer, and then cue into the current topic by relating it with what has gone before. At the same time, attempts should be made to arouse and sustain interest. We believe that the opening five minutes of each lesson are crucial for it is the moment of truth when the students decide whether to attend or not. One useful way to arouse interest at this stage is to pose a problem and invite solutions from the class, another is to open the lesson with a telling illustration, a loop film for example. At any rate, vague and rambling introductions should be avoided at all cost and since the introduction is crucial, it follows that it merits very careful preparation.

2. Development and Application

The lesson may proceed in several stages since at any particular stage the method of teaching will, as far as possible, be the one most suited to that time, that stage, and these students. Attempts should be made to build up a logical sequence of concepts and to make the whole a meaningful experience. To this end the teacher should give working examples, draw upon his own experience, give opportunities to discuss problems and freedom to experiment with things and ideas without fear of failure.

It is during this stage of the lesson that new knowledge is imparted and insightful learning takes place. And as a generalization, the teacher should lead the students from what they already know to the unknown, from the concrete to the abstract and from particular cases to general examples. As far as possible, every student's progress will be constantly monitored by questions and answers or by discussion. After each main point, there should be some recapitulation in which the class takes an active part.

3. Conclusion

Each lesson must have a fairly precise end, the students should know when the lesson has ended. The conclusion of the lesson should contain a lucid summary of what has been learned, and again, the students should take an active part in recalling it. Following the summary, the students might be given an introduction to the next topic together with sources of reference for preparatory reading if this is necessary. It is at this stage that the teacher should close the lesson and avoid letting it fizzle out in an indeterminate fashion. Above all the students should leave, knowing that they have had more success than failure, that they have worked hard and that they have learned.

DESIRABLE FEATURES TO INCLUDE IN A LESSON

1. Variety of presentation

This can give life to a lesson and changes in method can revive flagging interest. We can inject this new life by the use of aids, by question and answer tactics, by exercises and so on. But we can also do it by simply changing the vocal presentation. We may use a slow delivery to get across some very important matter on which we wish the student to take notes, perhaps followed by an increase in tempo when we give an illustration. There are even occasions when advantage may be had by seeming to talk to ourselves!

2. Emphasis on major points

In lesson planning, one of the most important strategic decisions to be made is which major matters need to be recalled after the lesson. These must be kept to a minimum. One useful method of making an emphasis is to repeat a sentence several times. Each time it is repeated the emphasis is shifted slightly. Thus, for example, 'learning is said to be a change in behaviour'. This followed by some expansion on the word behaviour, and then 'learning (pause), is a change in . . . what? . . . John?' then a few more sentences followed by 'learning is . . . what, . . . Ann?'. Not only does this aid immediate recall but, by suitable spacing it may be retained permanently. This is not the only way in which we can emphasize major issues, but it is both effective and useful. Crisp, slogan-like statements make for more useful cues for recalling lessons than complex technical sentences however erudite they may sound. An example of the latter given by J. McV. Hunt in the Open University Source Book *Personality growth and learning*, is the following:

'Perhaps, the task of developing proper motivation is best seen, at least in nutshell form, as limiting the manipulation of extrinsic factors to that minimum of keeping homeostatic need and exteroceptive drive low, in favour of facilitating basic information-processing to maximize accurate anticipation of reality.'

3. Student activity and participation

Learning, as we can see, is an active response to information. It is fallacious to assume that learning takes place when the student merely sits and hears the teacher, but learning does take place when the situation demands that the student *does* something. Learning is much more likely when there is active participation by the students. Not all subjects lend themselves to the use of exercises or problem solving, but it is still possible to encourage active participation through discussion, question and answer, debate and so on.

4. Feedback

Knowledge of results is vitally important to both learners and teachers. In almost any situation one can think of, we like to have some knowledge of how we are getting on. In learning, enthusiasm for a subject is often maintained by the learner deriving continuous satisfaction from the knowledge that he is coping with the situation. The teacher, too, gets feedback on his teaching by the response of the class and by the results of questions, exercises and tests. A wise teacher will not blame the

dullness of the students when the results are constantly dis-
appointing, but will first examine critically his own contribution
to their classroom performance.

5. Student success

This is very much related to the previous paragraph and is based
on the simple truth that success breeds success, whilst failure
destroys. We should make provision for the students to achieve
and to know they have achieved some degree of success. With
less able students we help them to feel they have succeeded well
at the essentials of the lesson — the MUST KNOW, whilst the
able ones can go on to the SHOULD KNOW and NICE TO KNOW
areas. It is very much a matter of knowing the students well, and
of reinforcing desirable behaviour. And this is particularly necessary when the students are finding difficulties.

6. Coping with fast and slow learners

(a) Fast learners may include those students with prior knowledge of the subject and in further education they are by no
means rare. Clearly, these students may become very bored and
lethargic if we expect them to proceed at the same pace as the
rest of the group. On the one hand, the teacher should not
assume that bright students have complete mastery of a subject;
he can check their knowledge by asking at least one fairly
complex and searching question during each lesson. On the
other hand the teacher must seek ways of ensuring that bright
students do not lose enthusiasm for the subject. One method is
to encourage them to undertake some personal research into an
interesting aspect of the subject whilst yet another would be to
encourage them to work in small groups with less able students
whom they can help.
(b) The slow learner presents quite a different set of problems.
There must be some provision for individual attention, possibly
during a personal tutorial. Here again, any success must be
quickly reinforced. The slow learner calls for much patience on
the part of the teacher who must accept the responsibility for
making the subject as comprehensible as possible for him.
Remember that facts are easier to learn than concepts and to

learn some facts correctly will provide a degree of motivation. Encouragement, tact and patience are the key-words.

7. Questioning

Questions must be chosen carefully and worded precisely and unambiguously. If they are questions of fact the answer should be precise; if they are about ideas they may give rise to a variety of points of view. In the latter case we should consider each contribution as likely to be reasonable and if an answer seems completely unrelated to the question, we should try to estabish how the student arrived at it and then re-direct him. Very often, seemingly stupid answers are the proper response to badly asked questions. In other words, we must not have a stereotyped expectancy when listening to answers but we must attempt to understand how the students are thinking. The teacher's attitude should encourage the students to try to answer, and we can do this by making them feel they are making worthwhile contributions to the lesson. The teacher should enjoy question and answer sessions and this, in turn, helps the student to relax. A sense of humour is useful so long as it is not inadvertently unkind. Young adults are particularly sensitive to sarcasm and find it destructive to their morale. One good rule is never to be sarcastic and never to laugh at a student's response unless it is funny enough for him to enjoy the joke. The functions of questioning may be any or all of the following: to discover present knowledge . . . to revise previous work . . . to set problems which lead into new subject material . . . to maintain interest and alertness . . . to encourage reasoning . . . to discover if students are understanding . . . to help them make observations . . . to draw inferences . . . to revise the main points of lessons . . . to pose further problems and to test the teacher's effectiveness.

8. Students' note-taking

Taking notes is a natural part of the student's day. The taking of notes has many advantages; it is impossible to remember all that has been said; we feel more satisfied if we can come away from a lesson with an accurate and creditable set of notes and, of course, notes are invaluable when revising for examinations. Teachers should encourage students to take notes only when it is necessary to do so. In further education, students often think they must write everything down verbatim, from the initial 'good-morning' to the final 'au revoir'. This note-taking sometimes seems to continue through anecdotes, digressions and talk about the weather. If students are too note-conscious some re-education is needed, and the teacher should clearly indicate the passages where note-taking is appropriate and those where it is not required.

If homework is set it should never call for a mere copying of part of the students' notes as this reinforces the belief that verbatim reports are desirable. Homework should, as a rule, ask the students to apply what they know to the solving of problems.

STRUCTURING A LESSON PLAN

Although lesson notes may be brief and arranged in any one of many ways, the teacher should have in his mind a kind of plan. The one given below includes the decisions which he should make in advance and their relationship to one another. It is not intended to be a model for the teacher's notebook.

SUBJECT OF LESSON:
CLASS LEVEL:
OBJECTIVE OF LESSON:

TIME	SUBJECT MATTER	METHOD	AIDS
0–5 min.	Recapitulation of previous lesson	didactic	
5–10 min.	Introduction of subject to direct attention	exposition	diagram
10–25 min.	New knowledge	exposition	O.H.P. Loop film
25–35 min.	Consolidation of major points	discussion	
35–45 min.	Recapitulation of subject matter Subject of next lesson	didactic	summary on chalkboard

Now if we put all this together we come up with some useful generalizations of which the really significant ones are these:

STUDENTS LEARN

1. *By association:* Begin with relevant previously learned material and associate new knowledge with it.
2. *By interest:* Encourage students to want to learn. Motivate through personal enthusiasm.
3. *By success:* Be generous with praise and gentle in criticism. Anticipation of further success motivates whilst anticipation of failure destroys the will to go on.
4. *By sequential development:* Make sure that the foundations for new knowledge are sound so that each stage develops from what is already understood.
5. *By understanding:* What the student learns must be meaningful to him. Repetition of definitions must not be confused with insight. Facts may be remembered but the teacher should test for the understanding of concepts and this goes beyond recalling facts which relate to concepts.
6. *By recapitulation:* We need to exercise what we know or our understanding will fade. This calls for regular recapitulation of previous knowledge.

In spite of all we do, in the end learning is idiosyncratic and dependent on the individual characteristics of each student. We cannot guarantee that students will learn from this method or that because we know there are times when our teaching methods seem in vain. We also know however, that by careful lesson planning we can, at least, minimize the risk of failing to teach effectively.

Lesson planning begins with our consideration of the learning environment. Our intentions and concern are built into our schemes of work and our lesson plans. We feel certain that learning is most efficient when lessons become works of art . . . and like any works of art they lean heavily on a background of scientific study.

Micro-training Exercise

Closing a lesson

Each group member to select the lesson he will teach in Unit Thirteen and write down its objective. He will then prepare the last three or four sentences with which he might close the lesson and these will conclude with a precise and emphatic statement of what the students know as a result of being taught this lesson. In this statement he should avoid any qualifications or expressions either of doubt or hope.

As he says this last sentence he will look at each group member and try to communicate to them that the lesson has been interesting and that he has enjoyed the company of his students. The lead-in sentence might refer to further study, to the next lesson, to the students' test results, and so on but this lead-in should be very brief since it normally follows the recapitulation stage.

Film

Closing a section of a lesson

Observe the teacher in this film and try to read the non-verbal signals with which he ends this part of the lesson. Fill in the rating scales below.

RESTATEMENT OF LESSON OBJECTIVE

Not stated.	Muddled and imprecise.	Clear to those who attended.	Clear to all students.	Precise and unambiguous.

Detracted from meaning of statements.	Distracting.	Gave support to statements.	Added interest to statements.	Emphasized precision and interest. Motivating.

Discuss each assessment in turn.

Unit 10

Study Session

Methods of teaching

There are a number of different methods of teaching but all of them are designed with two major objectives in view: to motivate the students to learn and to organize the subject matter to be appropriate to their needs.

Unfortunately our choice of method is riddled through with little and sometimes unpredictable variables. Some students learn better from methods they have come to expect us to use – they may indeed learn best by being worse taught. Some teachers come alive and radiate enthusiasm when they lecture but are restless and impatient in face-to-face situations. Some methods just won't fit into some rooms and so on. So we choose as wisely as we can. The more common methods are outlined briefly below.

Discussion   This has been described in *Unit Four*. It may be free or controlled by a leader. Unled groups tend to throw up leaders who may dominate and mislead the group. Leaders of controlled discussions should have an objective and should prepare, in broad outline, the course they want the discussion to follow. The leader should encourage the diffident but not demand participation, he should help the garrulous or domineering to learn to listen by reinforcing good listening habits. He should summarize the progress from time to time and recapitulate the main contributions at the end.

Discussion is useful for concept development and attitude

orientation and enables the teacher to know his students, their progress and their problems more fully.

Motivation should derive from the sense of freedom and participation, from interest in the subject itself and from the teacher's interest in his students' views.

The Lecture   This has been considered in minature in *Unit Seven*. It is a talk, with or without illustrations, or demonstrations, which is given relatively independently of the students' reactions or active participation. A good lecture is a highly sophisticated mode of presentation of which only a few teachers are capable and consequently it should be prepared with considerable care.

It should be accurately timed and, if necessary, rehearsed. Illustrations should be of professional quality and designed for the lecture, not copied from some other source for which they were appropriate. It should be 'talking' communication and not written matter being read out loud. It is economical of a lecturer's time and can be effective with very large groups. It is useful for presenting a person and his special knowledge to an audience.

Students should be prepared to hear the lecture, possibly by being given a position paper to read in advance. The handout given after the lecture should be succinct and immediately comprehensible in the light of what has gone before.

Lectures should generally be followed by seminars and tutorials or exercises in some form or another.

The ability to derive value from lectures is part of a professional man's repertoire of competencies and the discipline which underlies this ability is demanding. Unfortunately modern teaching methods tend to atrophy this essential ability to such a degree that many students are unable to enjoy the full advantage of membership of learned societies and radio talks: may the time be far off when we are forced to have dancing girls at symphony concerts!

The difficulty of learning from a lecture derives from the absence of *demand* for participative intellectual activity. Motivation derives from the conscious mental decision that the subject matter is of consequence to the student.

The lesson   This has been considered in *Unit Nine*. It is a session, so planned that at each stage of its development the method used is the one most likely to promote efficient learning. It invariably involves the participation of the students whose progress is constantly monitored by questions, discussion, exercises and practical activity. It is suitable for groups of up to about twenty although it can be used with groups of thirty.

In a lesson the responsibility for the students' progress rests with the teacher. He should have a clear objective and a lesson plan.

Motivation derives, in the last resort, from the ability of the teacher to motivate.

Demonstration   This may be a part or the whole of a lesson or lecture. It should be planned for students to SEE WHAT HAPPENS and the demonstration material should be so arranged and presented that the focal point of attention will be the place from which they will see the visual information they need (see *Unit Eleven*). No ancillary equipment should be visually dominant and no equipment should be allowed to distract attention when it is not being used (*Unit Six*).

Crucial to effective demonstration is the sequence of manipulative and verbal presentation. It should be so organized that the students verbally anticipate the steps that the demonstrator is going to take. Thus critical parts of statements should, in general, follow the action which they are intended to describe. This is emphasized by Galparin consequent upon his researches into teaching science and acknowledges the finding of Skinner and others as explained in *Unit Six*.

Basic to good demonstration is that the receivers perceive the messages the demonstrator intends to communicate. If it be, for example, the effect of moving a magnet into and out of a coil of wire as indicated by the movement of a galvanometer needle, the galvanometer should be set immediately above or below or very close to the coil so that the cause-effect connection can be seen and therefore perceived simultaneously. The two thus become intellectually connected through their contiguity to reinforce the theoretical implications of the process. Furthermore, the

magnet's poles should be visually differentiated — one, say, red
and the other black in order to give visual emphasis to the concept of the magnetic field of force. The sense of the current in
the windings too, may be visually emphasized with, say a white
paper arrow placed on them. The actual demonstration then
constitutes a direct cue to the principle being taught (Fig. 13).

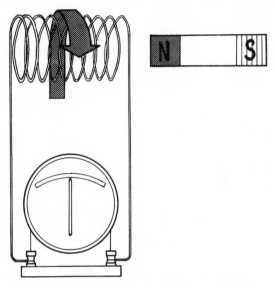

Fig. 13 A demonstration experiment

In demonstrating a skill the procedure also derives from the
perceptual objectives. If relevant it should be seen the right way
round — the learners should stand BEHIND a teacher demonstrating setting up a lathe or planing wood, for example. They
should first see the skill performed at the correct speed for long
enough to experience, at second hand, all the sensory impressions they can — the movement, the sound, the smell if there is
one, the environment. They should be seen as 'putting their
minds in the demonstrator's body'. At this stage the demonstrator should briefly give theoretical support to his movements —
'The weight of the body is transferred to the front foot to
enable us to keep the pressure of our left hand constant' and so
on. They will then be allowed to reflect on this for two or three
movements before any further explanation is given.

This should be followed by precise instructions for stance, sequence, safety measures and so on that MUST be known. These should be presented authoritatively with a view to conditioning the learner. Then any special details will be demonstrated at slow speed, the learners made to take up any special positions that are unnatural or to feel the effects of movements they need to experience.

As soon as reasonable they should begin to practice and as they do so only the minimum of guidance should be given and then always in a positive rather than negative manner: 'Try this' rather than, 'Don't do that'.

As the skill develops, the learners may be given supplementary demonstrations or watch loop films in order to retain their mental maps of good performance.

Exercises   These may be set as individual or group work. They should be realistic tasks based on the course work, and having set them the teacher should intervene only to give encouragement and to prevent frustration. The exercises must be designed to give students evidence of their progress — not evidence of their incompetency.

Exercises should, so far as possible, reflect all the objectives of the course. Consequently, in a subject that involves practical and theoretical components, the exercises should also include practical and theoretical work.

Exercises should be assessed immediately on completion and if possible the students themselves should go in for some form of self-assessment. Objective-type exercises are useful for monitoring theoretical learning since they can be marked in very little time. Students should always be clear about the criteria of assessment — in an essay are we looking for good writing, accurate spelling, grammatical accuracy, mature style, good story or imaginative writing, or some of each? And what matters most?

Laboratory Practical Work   This should be designed to promote the learning implied in the objective. If, as in Nuffield science, the processes which mediate the solution of problems are of more consequence than the solutions themselves the work will consist of a process of guided discovery with a great deal of thinking and discussion as well as doing. Galparin concluded in his work that practical activity tends to inhibit thinking, a finding that supports the need for time for reflection, for making intelligent proposals of hypotheses without fear of 'being wrong'. Indeed, insofar as science is a way of knowing based on the inductive method of reasoning, upon observation and the correlation of quantitative variables — there can be no wrong answers per se.

Tutorial Is a face to face meeting of the student and his teacher for testing and consolidating the student's progress and for listening to and helping him with his problems (whatever they may be). Demands should be severe but the communication mode should be sympathetic and collaborative. The student may be required to support his exercise period methods, present a brief paper or pre-prepared recorded tape and support it, or simply explain the reason for his difficulties (Fig. 14).

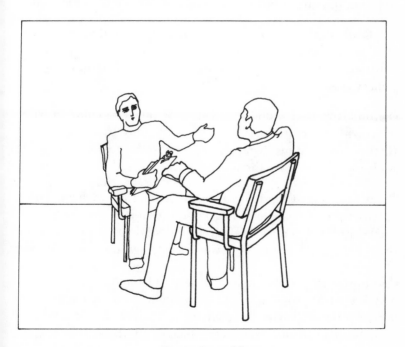

Fig. 14 A tutorial

Seminar   A small group meeting called to strengthen and clarify existing knowledge. It frequently follows a lecture but may stand on its own provided the group members have previous knowledge or experience of the subject matter. It may be opened by a student reading a brief paper and then by the group raising issues for further clarification. The teacher questions and — when necessary — explains. Pre-preparation is essential.

Other methods which should be known about at this stage and studied at leisure after the course are:

Project Method   This may be individual or group work. It consists of an investigation or development appropriate to the student's needs and interests, which he carries out with the minimum of tutorial guidance. It should call for appropriately high levels of initiative and imagination as well as ability and the student should be successful — if possible with some publicity.

The objective and its completion date should be quite clearly agreed at the outset but the method and form left to the student.

Syndicate Method   A problem situation is presented to a number of students who then, in separate small groups, arrive at solutions. These are then presented to the whole group in a plenary session.

Dalton Plan   Each student, individually, makes a contract with the teacher to master particular items of study by an agreed date. He then works at his own pace and chooses his own sequence of study and is tested by the teacher at the time of completion.

Team Teaching   Closely co-operating groups of teachers, with or without other assistance, have joint responsibility for the total learning of a number of groups of students. Usually consists of key presentation followed by small group work.

Case Study   Students examine at second hand a real or contrived event or problem and diagnose the reasons which led up to it or propose remedies for solving it. It gives opportunities for practise in solving 'human' problems and, through discussion, of attitude development.

It may give a false impression of the work role for which the teaching is designed. To give more realism the Incident Process method introduces the problem through an incident — a telephone call for example — and leaves the student to gather his own information from this beginning onwards.

Role Playing   Students act the role for which they are being trained, e.g. showroom salesmen, waiters, managers, interviewers, etc. Guidance and criticism should be given immediately and directed towards enhancing the student's confidence as well as improving the overt evidence of his performance.

Can be treated facetiously unless its purpose is evident and its value accepted. C.C.T.V. is useful in some of this work.

In-Tray   This is a form of role-playing in which the student is given a set of letters, files and documents such as he would have on the job. He attends to them under conditions which more or less simulate office working conditions and his approach, priorities and written work are assessed and discussed.

Business Games   Students play the roles of managers in a company the details of which they are given. The effects of their decisions are relayed back to them by a team of assessors and they take further action in the light of these effects. This can be useful teaching provided the students have faith in the assessors.

Micro-training

Opening a lesson

Each member of the group will present the opening of the lesson he intends to teach in *Unit Thirteen.* He will begin by stating his objective and writing a heading on the chalkboard or flip-chart. He will then outline the main stages in the content of the lesson in such a way as to motivate his students to want to be successful.

Each group member will prepare a verbalized rating scale

which shows the spectrum of motivation that might be experienced and he will show on it his reaction to the teacher. After each lesson the group members will give the teacher their assessments together with any suggestions they may have which could be helpful to him. Television will be used if it is available.

MICROTEACHING

So far in this course we have used micro-training methods. These, Len Powell introduced in 1959 as a way of initiating good presentation techniques in industrial training and because of their value he then used them at Garnett College as part of the induction training for teachers in Further Education.

In 1963, the concept of microteaching was introduced at Stanford University by Dwight W. Allen and others.[1] This is a more sophisticated tool which is valuable in initial teacher training, in continuous training and in research: in our opinion it should be preceded by micro-training experience and this view is being accepted fairly generally.

In essence, microteaching consists of short teaching periods with small classes, a follow-up critique session and a reteach period with a similar small class using revised and improved techniques which have been planned during and after the critique session. There are three microteaching modes — the micro-lesson, the micro-class and the research clinical session.

The micro-lesson　The objective of a micro-lesson is to develop a particular teaching skill such as, for example, the skill of asking and dealing with the responses to questions.

A typical sequence of events would be as follows:

1. The trainee-teachers are given a live or taped demonstration of the skill being used.

2. Each prepares a 5-minute lesson which rests heavily on the exploitation of this particular skill. He might, for example, set out to teach the concept of a river delta or a 3-start thread or the action of a ball-valve cistern.

3. He teaches this lesson to 3 or 4 *actual* students, his supervisor observes the lesson and it is video-taped.

4. The students and the supervisor fill in rating scales which the supervisor collects.

5. The trainee prepares the room for the next trainee.

6. The trainee and the supervisor discuss the lesson for 10-minutes with particular reference to the particular teaching skill being developed. In this they refer to the ratings and the video-taped record.

7. The trainee has 15-minutes in which the replan his lesson in the light of 6.

8. He teaches the recast lesson to a similar group as before.

9. The procedure 6. is repeated and the lessons compared. The total cycle takes 45 minutes.

The micro-class   This follows a few weeks after the start of micro-lesson training and the two techniques are continued side by side:

1. Three or four trainees together plan a 12-lesson unit of instruction with each lesson lasting from 20—25 minutes.

2. One trainee gives a lesson which is observed by his colleagues and by the supervisor. At the end of the lesson the trainees and the students fill in general feedback forms and forms for rating the particular teaching skill being developed.

3. The students leave and the trainees and their supervisor analyse the lesson and its ratings.

A total time of about an hour is devoted to the lesson and its critique.

One important outcome of the development of microteaching has been the adoption of a vocabulary to define certain teaching skills. The most important to us at this stage, all of which could be amplified, are sketched out below:

1. *Stimulus variation:* changes in method, non-verbal signals and questioning techniques designed to maintain motivation to learn.

2. *Set induction:* The procedure followed at the opening of a lesson to orientate the students towards learning the subject content.

3. *Closure:* Terminating a lesson or group of lessons so that

the new knowledge gained integrates with what was already known.

4. *Non-verbal cues:* Pauses, nods, smiles and so on that lead a student or a class to move towards understanding.

5. *Reinforcement skills:* Verbal and non-verbal reinforcements that tend to crystallize understanding.

6. *Fluency in questioning:*

7. *Probing questions:* Questions that test understanding as against rote responding.

8. *Higher-order questions:* Questions that demand the structuring of new ideas from what is known.

9. *Divergent questions:* Questions that require open-ended answering.

10. *Recognizing attending behaviour:*

11. *Illustrating and use of examples and analogies:*

12. *Planned repetition and sequencing:*

MICROTEACHING EXERCISE

The objective of this exercise is to introduce members to micro-teaching techniques. These should be more extensively exploited in follow-up courses.

Each group member to design a five-minute lesson for a group of three students (invited for the exercise). This should be designed to teach a single simple skill or a single concept. For a group of 12 members, a group of 12 students, four V.T.R. sets, four camera technicians, and one supervisor, the timetabling would be as shown on p. 125. This 75-minute period will be repeated twice to give all members an opportunity of practising. One observer in each group will pay attention to the activity interplay using the following scale as indicated:

Time in min.	0	1	2	3	4	5
Teacher talking to group						
Students talking to teacher or thinking						

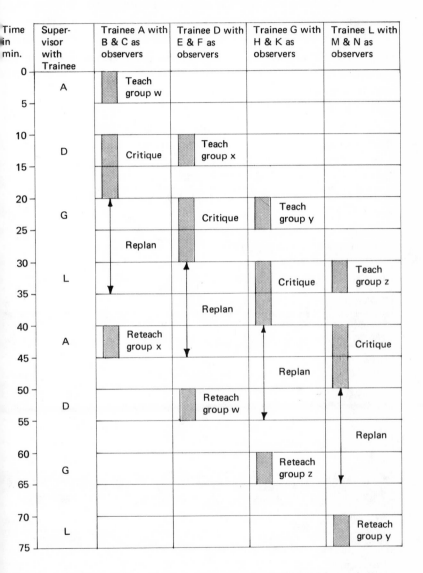

Time in min.	Supervisor with Trainee	Trainee A with B & C as observers	Trainee D with E & F as observers	Trainee G with H & K as observers	Trainee L with M & N as observers
0	A	Teach group w			
5					
10	D	Critique	Teach group x		
15					
20	G		Critique	Teach group y	
25		Replan			
30	L			Critique	Teach group z
35			Replan		
40	A	Reteach group x			Critique
45				Replan	
50	D		Reteach group w		
55					Replan
60	G			Reteach group z	
65					
70	L				Reteach group y
75					

Review session with each group separately followed by a full group meeting to consolidate what has been learned and plan the next session.

The other observer in each group will attend especially to one factor in both the teach and reteach sessions and each trainee will be assessed for a different skill. The scales will be as follows with a tick for a positive or useful exercise of the skill and a cross for an interference.

The students being taught will, after each micro-lesson, fill in the following scale.

The lesson was	Too simple	Easy to follow	Too difficult
I	Felt bored	Worked well	Was overworked
The teacher was	Unhelpful	Considerate	Very helpful

STIMULUS VARIATION

Time in min.	0	1	2	3	4
Talking					
Changing intonation					
Changing pace					
Prompting or cueing					
Questioning					

	0	1	2	3	4
Non-verbal signs					
Eye signals					
Hand signals					
Head signals					
Moving					
Smiling					
Listening					

SET INDUCTION   *Closure*

Time in min.	0	1	2	3	4	5
Clarifying objectives			Checking success			
Providing Gestalt			Recapitula-ting			
Challenging			Reinforcing			
Interesting			Encouraging			
Predicting success			Challenging			
Justifying			Further study			

NON-VERBAL CUES REINFORCEMENT SKILLS
PLANNED REPETITION AND SEQUENCING

Time in min.	0	1	2	3	4	5
N.V. Cueing —						
Eyes						
Movement						
Reinforcing —						
N.V.						
Verbal						
Repeating						
Sequencing						

QUESTIONING, RECOGNIZING ATTENTION AND ILLUSTRATING

Time in min.	0	1	2	3	4	5
Questioning fluency						
Probing questioning						
Higher order questioning						
Divergent questioning						
Recognizing attention						
Illustration						
Analogy						
Example						

REFERENCES

1. Allen, Dwight W., *Microteaching: A Description*. Stanford University School of Education publications, 1967.
2. Allen, Dwight and Ryan, Kevin, *Microteaching*. Addison-Wesley Publishing Company, Inc., Massachusetts 1969.

Unit 11

Study Session

Aids to teaching

It is an interesting fact that each new explosion of novelty in education and training produces a shock wave of success followed, so often, by a relaxation. The novelties are created and exploited first by the seekers around, the divinely discontented, who take a new thing in their hands and transform it into a star. But those who follow take the same thing in their hands and, too often, they find it is a burden without light.

One clue to the difference lies in the objectives which different teachers choose. There are those who, knowing that learning is an idiosyncratic experience, set out to provide their listeners with an inspiring intellectual environment and they see this as a total operation — inspiring in content, method and form: aesthetically unimpeachable as well as mechanistically accurate. They know by instinct or by training that 'showing a picture of the thing' is no more than the equivalent of reciting the pages of a textbook and so when they choose an aid they look at the facets of the communication it could support before they use it. The most significant of these facets are the function of the message, its creative qualities, its content and the process by which it is transmitted and received.

THE FUNCTIONS OF AIDS

Basically the function of an audio-visual message should be to stimulate particular responses in those who receive it. This implies that the teacher has diagnosed likely responses to different audio-visual messages and, in the light of this diagnosis, has prescribed the particular form he chooses both for its content and its mode. The function of the message may indeed be to show what something is like: to transcribe reality. If it is, the percepts it evokes should so far as possible be those evoked by the reality itself. This, as in a scientific demonstration may call for verilisimilitude or it may call for impressionism, and the latter can be a more direct source of valuable understanding than the former. When, for example, Utrillo painted a picture, he transcribed reality in such a manner that what he, and many others, received from his canvas was more truly what Utrillo knew of the reality than a photograph would have been.

Many communication aids are designed to fulfil this function in which the most important quality should be fidelity to the reality they seek to transcribe — fidelity so far as the sensory impressions they evoke are concerned. Thus, if a teacher refers to the music of Bach and supports what he says by playing a record, he is using an aid which transcribes reality and it does so with equal reliability whether it is a mono or a stereo recording. But the fidelity of the sensory impression received from the stereo recording is greater than that from the mono one: this faithfulness of the message that reaches the receiver's brain and not the technical accuracy of the transcription is the significant characteristic of the aid. Thus in talking of buildings or tennis strokes the lecturer might use film since we see buildings as we move and tennis strokes are themselves movement; in talking of finger prints or circuits he might use transparencies or charts and in talking of Spanish or music he might choose stereo recordings. He chooses with a mind to the psychological consequences of his choice.

But not all aids are intended to transcribe reality. Some are used to catalyse conceptual activity and this is not a bad thing even if the subject is a scientific one. Suppose, for example, a lecturer shows that when white light passes through a blue glass it turns blue and then, without waiting to hear the answer, asks why this happens. By so doing he may evoke the scientifically reliable conclusion that the glass absorbs light of all colours except blue. But on the other hand he might stir the dreamings of a Shelley:

> 'Life, like a dome of many coloured glass,
> Stains the white radiance of eternity
> 'Til death shatters it to fragments'.

thoughts that more than compensate for the loss of scientific plausibility.

Here, the role of the message has been to catalyse: to trigger off psychological activity. Here the message began an active response by the initiatives of imagination, a reaching for creativity, and in responding to our creative capacities in this way we may transcend the reality we experience.

The teacher may indeed choose his aid deliberately to contribute towards affective responses. If he is successful the response which is evoked will grow from the rapport between him and his students: this will, as it were, clear away the obstacles to affective and aesthetic perception.

THE CONTENT OF AIDS

So first a teacher chooses an aid for its function — what it is intended to *do*. He then examines it for its content, the amount and variety and complexity of the information it contains, the way this information is transmitted and the reciprocal support it needs from the teacher. Many aids are full of information, particularly photographs, and cine films, but this alone is no drawback to understanding provided they effect a psychological unity. Aids that give rise to too many psychological processes on the other hand detract from understanding. Thus, for example, a photograph of a market place teeming with life could communicate simply an understanding of the physical reality of that particular scene. If, on the other hand, the picture included a monkey stealing fruit from a stall, a beggar with no legs dragging himself along with his hands, a dealer beating a donkey with a cudgel and a child balancing on the edge of a roof, the message might well be submerged under the weight of interpretative and creative activity to which the picture gave rise. It is wise, before using an illustration to ask an appropriate person to say what the picture shows.

SPECIFIC OBJECTIVES

Within these general objectives are contained more specific ones. An aid may be used simply to help the listeners to listen more willingly, to make the occasion more pleasant or aesthetically more interesting: a seemingly vague objective but one which is real enough when it is experienced. Another aid may be used to make words more comprehensible or less ambiguous and yet another may be designed to attract the attention of the audience. Indeed, attracting attention is easy enough. A loud noise, a bright light, a weird picture and so on will attract attention, but this alone is not enough: the aid that does this and no more, is not an end in itself, it is an invitation that has been accepted and it places on the lecturer the responsibility for providing ideas that are consequential enough to justify the effort implicit in his students' response.

Some sequence of ideas are difficult to follow and yet impossible to simplify and as a result, listeners have difficulty in controlling their attention. In these circumstances, an aid can assist as a visual focus as well as being a complement to the verbal message. Quantitative relationships may be difficult to comprehend unless they are supported graphically.

So in designing material to supplement a lecture it is important to ask how it will cause the audience to respond — what will it make them *do* — what behavioural objective has the teacher in mind when he chooses to use it. Does he want to use it to:

invite co-operation
explain a word
attract attention
hold attention
illustrate relationships
challenge his listeners to think or act
consolidate what he has said?

If the lecturer has one such an objective in mind he will use the illustration with greater precision, greater force and, consequently, more effect.

LECTURING AIDS

The basic aids which a teacher may use are the flat surfaces on which he can write or draw diagrams and pictures. Chalkboards are convenient for this purpose; they come in a variety of forms, colours and sizes and if a board is well used the immediacy of the message displayed on it and its close association with the speaker himself contribute considerably to the acceptability of what he says.

There are two alternatives to the chalkboard; the white board (or any other coloured plastic surface) and the flip-chart which is a pad of paper sheets measuring some two feet wide by three feet long clipped together at their top edges. Water based felt writers can be used on either of these surfaces giving clear brightly coloured writing. Unfortunately the squeaking of felt on the writing surface can be irritating and this drawback is more obvious to the students than it is to the teacher. Large wax crayons on the other hand, although they do not give such bright colours, write smoothly and silently on paper and may commend themselves to those who dislike felt writers.

Where the teacher intends to support his introduction by writing a main heading followed by a few sub-headings to which he will refer from time to time, a flip-chart is ideal. It is small enough not to be a distraction. He might then use a chalkboard or a white board for explanations and jottings which, having served their purpose, will be erased (Fig. 15).

Flip-chart illustrations can, of course, be pre-drawn and un-covered when they are needed. Alternatively, if the chart paper consists of blank newsprint, illustrations can be prepared in hard pencil, and then although they will be invisible to students, they will be quite clear to the teacher who can go over them with a crayon or pen when he is ready to do so.

It is critical to the total impact of a lesson that any material on view at the end should either summarize the lesson or empha-size its main theme. If details are left on view they will seem to be more significant than they should.

Pre-prepared illustrations may consist of charts, maps or dia-grams. They can be uncovered at the proper time and then removed from view afterwards. Charts should be selected with

Fig. 15 Writing surfaces

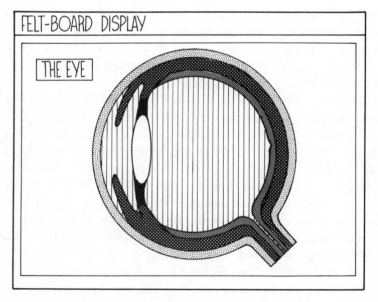

Fig. 16 Felt-board display made by layering felt cut-outs

care since they often carry too much information and too little visual emphasis of what is important.

Greater emphasis and selection is possible with felt-board illustrations. These are particularly suitable for lessons about a series of items or a sequence of events since the components of the display can be mounted in stages to fit the talk. Figures 16 and 17 show two displays of this kind.

FELT-BOARD DISPLAY

Fig. 17 Felt-board display in flock paper

Felt-board illustrations are usually made on drawing paper which is then backed with a special flock paper made for the purpose: it is possible to make the illustrations directly on flock paper itself but since it is not paper of a high quality, it is not particularly suitable for amateur artists who make generous use of an eraser. The backcloth can be of any suitable colour and should be stretched on its supporting board to eliminate any creases and then brushed with a wire (or very stiff) brush in order to roughen the felt surface.

Magnetic boards may be used in place of felt ones but they imply a different kind of image: the felt gives a very pleasing, gentle and often elegant impression whilst a magnet board, onto which the pieces snap with mechanical precision, gives a more practical and businesslike one. The components of the illustration can be moved around and taken off and put back on again without any fumbling or difficulty whatever, and this makes the board very suitable for diagrams which need changing by stages: playing chess, traffic control, moving mechanisms, architectural arrangements and so on.

Magnetic boards are usually wooden boards surfaced with a thin sheet of iron or tinplate. The pieces that fix onto them are made of anything that is convenient – paper, card, plywood or they may even be toy models, small tools and so on – and they have magnets stuck onto their back surfaces. Figures 18 and 19 show two magnet-board displays.

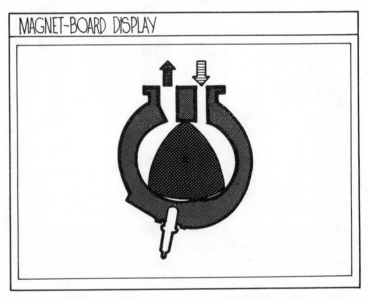

Fig. 18 Magnet-board illustration of the principle of the Wankel engine

There are other devices and techniques for displays of this kind but the feltboard and magnetic board represent the two alternative kinds of presentation that display surfaces make possible.

Displays of actual objects may be used in some lessons. If the objects are fairly small — fossils, instruments, packages and so on, they may be arranged on display shelves on a peg board background or on a specially prepared display stand for closer viewing later on. In this case, pre-prepared labels stuck into place at the same time as the object is displayed will assist in making the visual information more valuable as a summary of the talk.

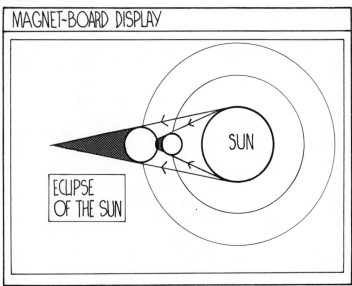

Fig. 19 Magnet-board display on drawn background

DEMONSTRATION MATERIALS

Generally speaking a demonstration is designed to let people *see* something although, of course, some are intended to appeal to senses other than sight. There are three main groups of demonstration exemplified by a cake being iced, an amoeba under a microscope displayed on a television monitor and an electromagnet being switched to show electromagnetic induction. Each of these has a different objective: the first sets out to show HOW something is done, the second to show WHAT something is like and the third is concerned with WHY something happens the way it does. More fundamentally they are concerned with communicating information about a skill, a fact and a concept respectively.

does. More fundamentally they are concerned with communicating information about a skill, a fact and a concept respectively.

The focal point of a demonstration should be the information centre — the place where the purpose of the demonstration happens. The demonstrator should perform and speak in such a way as to direct attention to this centre and there should be no ancillary equipment on view that has greater visual appeal to distract attention. It would be most unwise for a science teacher to demonstrate the working of a dynamo by driving it with a beautiful model triple expansion steam engine.

Not only this, but the students should be helped to discriminate between the bits and pieces wherever confusion is possible. Thus, for example, in demonstrating an Ohm's law relationship of some sort a teacher might use both a voltmeter and an ammeter — instruments indicating quite different things. But all too often there is hardly any way of telling the two instruments apart except by reading their scales, and at some distance this may not be easy. Furthermore, since they are joined into the circuit by leads, they can be stood anywhere; the voltmeter may be roughly where the ammeter is shown in the teacher's diagram and vice versa. Consequently some care is needed to make the demonstration clear. The important circuit components might be made visually dominant by means of cardboard labels and they can be arranged to correspond to a circuit diagram nearby. This is shown in Fig. 20 where, in particular, the tiny resistor, R, which is really the key character is the performance, is mounted on a background drawn to imply a resistor.

Where supporting equipment is likely to attract attention away from the information focus, it should either be concealed entirely or concealed and replaced by a less significant label. Thus a vacuum pump might be fitted into a cupboard and represented on the bench by a small box labelled 'Pump'. Alternatively the vacuum line could be labelled 'To vacuum pump'.

THE OVERHEAD PROJECTOR

Of all the devices available for supporting teaching of almost any kind, the overhead projector is the most versatile. It can be used clumsily, of course, and its full potential is realized only after

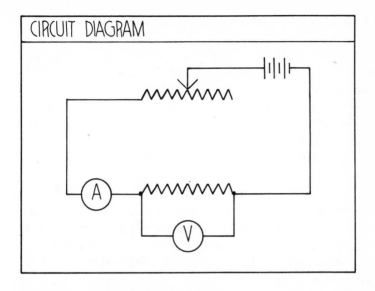

CIRCUIT DIAGRAM

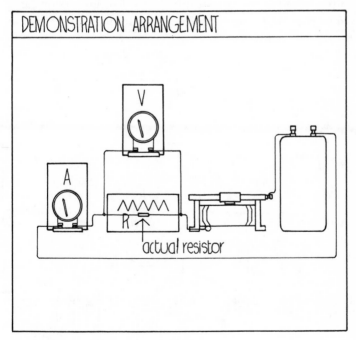

DEMONSTRATION ARRANGEMENT

actual resistor

Fig. 20

practice, but well-used it can be a most powerful and persuasive tool.

It requires no blackout and consequently should be properly positioned relative to the teacher and the class. It is usually best to suspend its screen high up across the teacher's right hand corner so that it slopes forward to meet the axis of the projector beam at right angles (Fig. 21). Most overhead projectors give an image of about five feet square at a distance of eight feet from the screen but some have short focal length lenses that give an image of the same size at about six feet distance. This means that the instrument used in the manner illustrated will be to the left of the line of view of any centrally placed display surface and out of the way of the main summary area on the right. The transparency surface is about 250 mm (10 inches) square and for the most comfortable use should be situated roughly level with the user's elbow.

If a teacher uses any form of projector for illustration he should be prepared at least for the lamp to burn out. This can

Fig. 21 Position of overhead projector screen

be overcome by replacing the lamp, a procedure which generally takes two or three minutes, but some overhead projectors are fitted with a built-in spare lamp that can be moved into place by means of a lever switch. For very important occasions, a spare projector connected to a separate electric socket is very reassuring.

The easiest things to use on an overhead projector are objects themselves: fern leaves, for example, look surprisingly beautiful on the screen, but small tools, dishes of liquid used for chemistry demonstrations, twigs to demonstrate pruning, small gear wheels and a fair range of other items can be used as they are. Similarly, silhouettes cut from card or paper may be projected onto the screen and, of course, moved around if they need be.

Notes can be written on transparent film and most projectors are fitted with a roll of acetate intended for use in this way. Acetate will accept a limited range of writing materials — some felt and fibre pens are suitable, as are certain waxy pencils and some coloured inks.

It is usually best to pre-prepare illustrations. These can be 'drawn' by scratching with a pointed instrument, drawn with black or coloured inks which are especially made for this kind of work, built up from self adhesive film, tapes or letters, photo-copied by one of a variety of methods or purchased ready printed.

In use, they may be presented as they are, simply as pictures, or they may be overlaid with film and supplemented with marks made on them during display. They can also be built up stage by stage by using overlays (Fig. 22), or disclosed stage by stage by using paper masks. Two parts of a diagram may be moved rela-tive to one another by drawing each on a separate sheet of film and sliding or rotating one on the other. Even working models made from Perspex and other materials can be used.

When a transparency is shown, whether from an overhead projector or any other source the students will want to look at it and the teacher should give time for this preliminary survey. With simple graphical material this may call for a pause of only a second or two but where the picture evokes creative psycho-logical processes he should postpone his intervention for perhaps

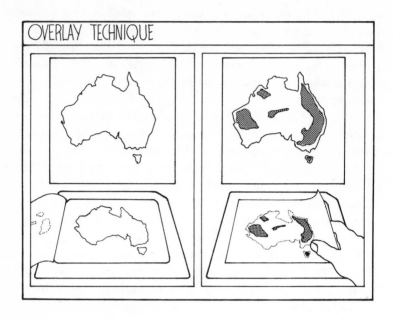

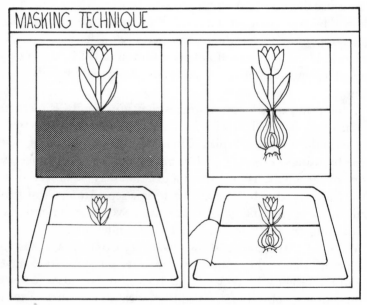

Fig. 22 Overhead projector transparency techniques

ten or even twenty seconds. His first statement may be designed
to postpone speaking for even longer, 'I wonder what you make
of that?', for example.

Closed circuit television is useful to teachers who need something more flexible than an episcope to show small objects or
delicate procedures on a large scale. It may be used too to present
video taped material or even to relay visuals and activities from
outside the room. The special physical qualities of television are
its silence of operation and the self-contained nature of the
equipment: the image comes from inside the monitor in a truly
face-to-face fashion. This influences the psychological quality of
the message — the facility with which it can imply immediacy
even if the material is video-taped. Because of this, the quality
of the image is less likely to be criticized than that of a projected
image on a screen where the transparency has obviously been
pre-prepared and should therefore be free from flaws.

But whatever device is used the basic principle remains: its
effectiveness as a communications device will depend a great
deal upon the teacher knowing what it is intended to *do* to his
students and then working with it towards that particular objective. And the difficulty he has in doing this increases as the
equipment becomes more automatic — with a full-length film he
becomes a member of the audience and loses his identity as a
leader.

SUMMARY

An aid should be regarded as an aid to effective communication.
The audio-visual message has a function, a content and a form
and these should be assessed in terms of total psychological
impact. It may be used to —

    invite co-operation

    explain words

    attract attention

    hold attention

    illustrate relationships

    challenge

    consolidate.

Aids to teaching include:
  Writing and drawing surfaces — chalkboards, etc.
  Display surfaces — feltboards, etc.
  Displays and demonstrations.
  Overhead projector.
  Slide transparencies.
  Tape recorder.
  Record player.
  Films.
  Television.
  Broadcasts.

Practical Exercise

Visual aids workshop

Each group member will prepare two visual aids, a transparency for the overhead projector and one other aid to be used in the lesson to be given in *Unit Thirteen.*

Micro-training

Presentation of a visual aid

Each group member will present each of his two visual aids to the group in the way he intends to use them in *Unit Thirteen.*
  Each member will write down what he believes the teacher intended the aid to do — the objective. Each aid will be discussed under the following headings:
  Impact of the visual message.
  Design quality.
  Appropriateness.

Unit 12

Exercise

Preparation of a lesson

Each group member will prepare a lesson to last for between 15 minutes and 25 minutes. The exercise or practical activity component of the lesson should be foreshortened to fit into the timing.

In preparing the lesson the following sequence should be followed:

1. Write down the objective of the lesson in behavioural terms.

2. Prepare the test to be used after the lesson in order to assess its success and state the maximum number of errors that you can allow.

3. State the age and status of the students for whom the lesson will be designed.

4. Write down the very few main steps in the lesson.

5. Prepare the aids, exercise sheets and handouts and check the existence and state of equipment you wish to use.

6. Prepare the lesson notes.

It is critical to allow for tactical variations during the lesson. Remember that learning is an idiosyncratic activity and that the method of teaching used at any moment should, theoretically, be the most appropriate one for the problems of that moment.

Here is an example of such a lesson preparation.

1. *Objective.* At the end of the lesson, every student will correctly translate the first nine numbers in Exercise (*c*) from decimal to binary notation within five minutes and be able to explain how he did it.

EXAMPLE OF LESSON NOTES

TO TEACH THE RUDIMENTS OF THE BINARY SYSTEM

Group: Technicians: Age 16 years

Time: 25 minutes

Reasons for Method		Matter	Method	Illustration
Introduction giving a general idea of the whole and to motivate through interest.		Recap of previous lesson. 'On-off' devices. Computers. Binary.	Questions, answers and explanations.	Chalkboard heading.
Development. Behaviourist — rote learning for success.	2	'On-off' representation of numbers.	Educe from group: rote learning by Q & A. Student participation.	Magnetic board
To provide data for concept formation.	6	Exercise on powers of two (a).	Class to complete duplicated exercise: individual help.	Duplicated sets of exercises.
Consolidation of data.	10	Powers of two in series (b).	ditto.	ditto.
Concept formation.	12	Binary series.	Educe by Q & A and recap.	Magnetic board.
Application: possibility of serious regression through initial failure.	16	Exercise in translation (c).	Class to complete duplicated exercises: individual help. Recap.	Duplicated sheets of exercises.
	21	Students to give binary symbols for 15, 17 and 32.		
Recapitulation and Consolidation through enjoyment, activity and implications of relevance.	25	Computer to add 15 and 17 and obtain 32.	Role playing using six students as components of computer.	

EXAMPLES

(a) **Complete the following:**

1. $2 \times 2 \times 2 = 2^3 = 8$
2. $2 \times 2 \times 2 \times 2 = 2^4 = 16$
3. $2 \times 2 \times 2 \times 2 \times 2 = 2^5 = \ldots$
4. $2 \times 2 \times 2 \times 2 \times 2 \times 2 = 2^{\cdots} = 64$
5. $2 \times 2 \times 2 \times 2 \times 2 \times 2 \times 2 = 2^{\cdots} = \ldots$
6. $2^2 = \ldots$
7. $2^{\cdots} = 256$

1. *Fold back along this line*

2. *Fold back along this line*

(b) **Complete the following:**

1. $2^{\cdots} = 1$
2. $2^{\cdots} = 2$
3. $2^2 = 4$
4. $2^3 = 8$
5. $2^{\cdots} = 16$
6. $2^{\cdots} = 32$
7. $2^6 = \ldots$
8. $\ldots = \ldots$
9. $\ldots = \ldots$
10. $\ldots = \ldots$

(c) **Complete the following:**

1.	2 = □□□■□ =	10		10
2.	5 = □□□■□■ =	101		101
3.	4 = □□□□□□ =			100
4.	9 = □□■□□■ =	1001		1001
5.	16 = □□□□□□ =			10000
6.	17 = □□□□□□ =			10001
7.	10 = □□□□□□ =			1010
8.	23 = □□□□□□ =			10111
9.	7 = □□□□□□ =			111
10.	514 = □□□□□□ =			1000000010

2. *Test.* Exercise (c) on exercise sheet following. Only one error will be allowed and that only No. 10.

3. *Target Students.* 16 year old technicians following a part-time day release course.

4. *Main Steps.* Opening: powers of 2 series: binary notation: recapitulation.

5. *Aids, etc.* Exercise sheet — given later.
   Tinplate sheet 0·5 m x 100 mm divided into six compartments with 6 wood tags fitted with disc magnets.
   Numbers 1, 2, 4, 8, 16, 32 on card 0·5 m x 300 m with tape to hang over students' necks.

6. *Lesson Notes.* The first column under *Reasons for Method* would not normally be included. The exercise sheet is folded as shown so that the students first see only the examples (a) They then turn the sheet over and work through examples (b) and then (c). Finally they can open it up to check their

answers. No. 10 of (c) is included for the quick workers who will need to extend the diagram of the panel before they can solve the problem.

Unit 13

Practical Exercise

Presenting a lesson

Each student will present his lesson and test for its effectiveness. The following check list should be used as a guide for discussion:

1. Were the *aims and objectives* of the lesson perfectly clear?
2. Was the subject developed within the limitations of the *time allowed?*
3. *Amount of material* — too much, too little, or just right?
4. Were *essential points* emphasized?
   Was any unnecessary material included?
5. Did the teacher *discover, explain and illustrate* points of difficulty?
6. Did the teacher promote and maintain *interest?*
7. Were *questions* framed to stimulate thought?
   Were questions well distributed around the group?
8. Did the teacher *summarize or recapitulate* by stages?
9. *Teaching aids*
   (*a*) Was the blackboard used adequately, clearly and neatly?
   (*b*) Were the pre-prepared aids appropriate and used effectively?
   (*c*) Was the demonstration equipment appropriate and used effectively?
10. *Speech.* Was the voice —
   (*a*) audible?   (*b*) interesting?
11. *Manner and approach*
   (*a*) Was class discipline satisfactory?

    (*b*) Was the teacher's personality (enthusiasm, approach-
ability, encouragement) appropriate?

    (*c*) Had he any *distracting* mannerisms?

12. (*a*) *Overall performance*
(Underline) Excellent/Above average/Average/Below
average/Poor

    (*b*) *Overall value.* Was the lesson a useful educative
experience?

Other comments

Each course member should be prepared to answer the following questions after presenting his lesson:

1. What did your students learn?

2. How do you know?

3. Could they have learned more by any other method?

4. Was this what you had in mind anyway?

Module IV

Preparing learning packages

Unit 14

Study Session

Programmed learning

It is not our intention to describe the procedures followed by professional programme writers in producing texts since this is a subject for long study: our objective is to teach how to produce written instruction, so sequenced and expressed that students learn from it. In the course of writing a — quite properly called — programme, you will think deeply and variously about how students learn and this is a useful bonus in itself.

B. F. Skinner of Harvard, consequent upon researches with animals and birds, concluded that learning should be broken down into very small steps so that when, after each step, the learner was required to express what he had learned, at least ninety-five per cent of his responses would be correct and also that he should know immediately upon responding whether he was right or not. This is the stimulus — response — reinforcement sequence of operant conditioning and forms the basis of what is known as linear programming. A most important characteristic of this type of programme is that each response is an integral part of the process of learning.

It should be remarked here that overexposure to programmed learning can cause an antipathy to the method simply because the learner becomes lonely.

A programme then is a coherent body of knowledge presented in such a way that, even in the absence of a teacher, a learner for whom it is intended will want to learn it and will be successful in doing so. The most basic programme that fits this definition is exemplified by the instructions on a beer-can on how to get it open — motivation, cue, stimulus, response and reward are immediately evident. Of course, the programme is unnecessary for the experienced opener of cans and inappropriate for the non-drinker of beer, and in life, this all works out as it should.

Most important is the fact that if the programme doesn't work and the motivated hopeful is unable to learn how to open the can he will buy a different brand of beer in future. This is validation of the tooth and claw type — succeed or get out!

However, in the quieter vistas of education and training it is easy to overlook these basic elements in organizing material for learning and if they are overlooked the programme suffers. The necessary steps which the programme writers should take then, are these:

1. *Define the objective* in behavioural terms giving, if necessary, the conditions under which the learner will demonstrate his knowing and the lowest standard of performance that will be acceptable.

2. *Write the terminal test.* This will be designed to show whether the learner has reached the required standard to have succeeded.

3. *Plot the learning sequence* by analysing the task to be learned. This will clarify intermediate sub-objectives.

4. *Write the programme.*

5. *Validate* it and revise it where necessary (Fig. 23).

DEFINING THE OBJECTIVE

This is the pivot of the whole exercise: it is a statement of the behaviour of the successful learner: it is a prescription for mastery. Not only is the objective essential to the programme writer but it can be of critical value to the learner.

In experiments in industrial training it has been found that in certain special cases the most efficient learning can result from doing *no more* than giving trainees a precise statement of their learning objective together with an example of the kind of terminal test they will be required to pass. The trainees are told

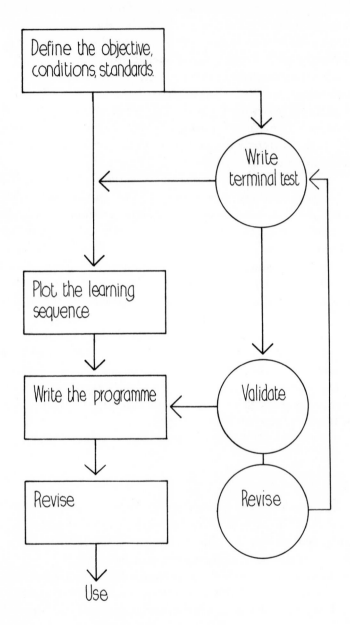

Fig. 23 Programme preparation

they can find out what they need to know by any means they choose.

This has its counterpart in the Dalton Plan in education. Here the learner makes a contract with his teacher to reach a certain standard by a certain date and is then free to learn how and when he will. Here, however, his progress and behaviour are constantly observed and, if necessary, modified by the teacher.

However, a programme *could* consist of a precise statement of the objective together with an example of the form of the terminal test or the test itself. For example:

PROGRAMME

You will learn to soft-solder together two given pieces of tin-plate, taking no longer than 12 minutes to do so. The joined pieces will form a circular disc that cannot be pulled apart by hand and so joined that there seems to be no thickness of solder within the joint. The solder flow from the joint will nowhere exceed a distance of 0·2 mm. You will use an electric soldering bit.

If you are not entirely sure what to do, write down your question and ask it of the instructor. When you have completed the test piece he will ask you these questions back again and you must answer them correctly. Go on practicing until you are ready to be tested.

TEST

The disk will be measured. It must be circular within the limits of ± 0·08 mm and the solder flow must not exceed 2 mm. The thickness over the lap must nowhere exceed 1·20 mm. You will be required to complete the work from start to finish in 12 minutes.

The fact that a well formulated objective on its own will sometimes cause learning to be as efficient as possible, highlights the importance of this stage.

Not all objectives are as easy to define as that given in the previous example but, as in the example, they all involve finding out what it is that a trained practitioner is able to do and how it is that he can do it. For instance, suppose we want to prepare a programme on the geology of the South-East of England we would begin by talking to, or at least, visualizing somebody who 'knows' the geology of the South-East of England at the level that we want our students to reach by the end of the programme. We would then decide what it is that he can do to reassure us that he 'knows'. He might, for example, recognize a map of the outcrops, be able to collect and identify the zone fossils, integrate what he knows in answering a series of objective-type questions on the ecology of the area, drill out a core and identify and describe the main chemical and physical properties of the samples and so on.

Of course, in designing a programme to teach a car owner how to change a wheel the business of clarifying the objective is pretty simple. But even here decisions have to be made. Do we want him to be able to change the wheel on his own car, on any type of car, or on goods vehicles? Do we expect him to be able to use only his own jack, or any jack? And so on.

THE TERMINAL TEST

This should be so designed that those who are able to do whatever is stated in the objective and who satisfy the conditions and minimum standards laid down there will pass: those who do not will fail. The test should therefore be validated to ensure that it satisfies these conditions. To do this, set the test to some forty or more students containing about half who are known to know and about half who do not know. The test should produce results which support more detailed and lengthy procedures for obtaining this information.

PLOTTING THE LEARNING SEQUENCE

This, basically, involves deciding the order in which the material is best learned. The car owner, for example, would best begin by learning how to change wheels on his own car since the motivation to do so is very strong and before doing so he needs to know nothing which can be learned more easily elsewhere. The embryo geologist might first learn to recognize the materials which comprise the main secondary and tertiary stratae of the area and end by considering alternative theories of the evolution of the rock formations. In general the sequence to each sub-objective works upwards through the learning hierarchy from S-R-R learning to concept learning and principle learning but achieves this very largely through S-R-R means. In general each sub-objective should develop from what has gone before and be necessary to the step that follows it.

WRITING THE PROGRAMME

The programme should take such a form that the learner works through it automatically — his mind should be entirely on the learning and not partially occupied with the mechanics of making the right moves, as it were. Generally it will require the learner to move forward in small steps and provide him with knowledge of his progress immediately after each step. Thus, consecutive frames might look like this:

Frame		Response
16	Food is unlikely to act as a reinforcer to an animal which is not	
17	If the animal's response is not followed by reinforcement, future similar responses will be made . . . . frequently	hungry
18	The animal is more likely to respond in the required fashion if each correct response is immediately	less
		reinforced

Here, the learner covers the frames beneath the one he is reading, writes in his response (a constructed response) moves his paper mask down one frame and when he does so he can see the correct response which he should have made in the right-hand column. Being right is a reinforcer and also serves to maintain the student's motivation.

VALIDATION

Before the programme is used extensively it should be tried out and, if necessary, modified. To this end, a group of, say twelve, students is selected and given a pre-test: this is usually the terminal test, or one very much like it, and those who fail the test are given the programme. It is clearly useless to present a programme to a learner who already knows what it is designed to teach: he will not be motivated and, on the contrary, will probably develop an antipathy for this mode of learning. Whilst the students work through the programmes an 'average' student is observed closely and any major hesitations he makes are noted. These are discussed with him after he has completed his work and the programme revised in the light of any important findings that may emerge. Next, the results are plotted on a chart, with errors marked by a cross, as follows:

Frame Number

Student	1	2	3	4	5	6	7	8	9	10	11	12	13	14	15	16	17	18	19	20	21	22	23
1																							
2											x												
3			x		x	x					x	x	x				x		x	x	x	x	x
4																							
5											x												
6											x			x									
7																							
8											x												
9											x					x							
10																							
11											x												
12																							

The example given shows evidence of a well constructed programme in which frame 11 needs rewriting or supplementing. It also shows that the programme was unsuitable for student No. 3 If, now, all the students except No. 3 pass the terminal test, the programme, with its modified frame 11, will be tested again to check the new insertion and then released for general use.

The principles discussed so far are now exemplified in the following sequence showing the preparation of a programme to teach Faraday's laws of electromagnetic induction.

PROGRAMME ON FARADAY'S LAWS OF ELECTRO-MAGNETIC INDUCTION

Objective: To be able to describe without hesitation, the electro-magnetic induction effects which occur when a bar magnet moves relative to a coil of wire.

To be able to relate as a proportionality the magnitude of an induced e.m.f. to its cause.

To use the terms *induction* and *flux* in their correct context.

Target Student: Has successfully followed a general electricity course through Ohm's law and basic circuitry.

Terminal Test:

Complete the following:
1. When a magnet moves relative to a coil of wire an_____ _____ _____ is _____ in the wire.
2. An e.m.f. is_____ in a coil whenever the_____ through the coil is_____ .
3. When a magnet is moved relative to a coil, the magnitude of the induced e.m.f. increases as the:
   (a)_____
   (b)_____
   (c)_____
4. The magnitude of an induced e.m.f. is proportional to the _____of change of _____ .
5. Draw a diagram of the arrangement used in the experiment.

Task analysis:

1. Connect together the circuit as instructed.
2. Move a magnet relative to a stationary coil and observe that a current flows only whilst the magnet moves.
3. Know this as the induced current.
4. Move the coil relative to the stationary magnet and observe that a current is induced only whilst the coil is moving.
5. Know that, whether or not a current is induced, an e.m.f. is induced when a coil and magnet are moved relatively to each other.

6. Predict that if they move together no e.m.f. is induced in the coil.
7. Observe that, all else being equal, the induced e.m.f. is greater for two adjacent similar poles than for one pole and that this, in turn, is greater than for two adjacent dissimilar poles.
8. State that the induced e.m.f. is caused by the change of magnetic flux.
9. Observe that for very slow relative motion the magnitude of the induced e.m.f. is less than for quicker relative motion.
10. State that the magnitude of the induced e.m.f. is increased by increasing the rate of change of flux.
11. Observe that, all else being equal, the e.m.f. induced in a coil of more turns is greater than that induced in a coil of fewer turns.
12. State that the induced e.m.f. is dependent on the rate of change of flux-turn linkages.

This analysis shows a steady progression through the learning hierarchy from multiple discrimination through a series of concepts to principles with each learning stage developing from the previous one. It also throws up a series of sub-objectives which must be achieved as the learning proceeds. For example, step 3 translated into behavioural terms becomes —
Be able to state that the galvanometer is deflected by an induced current.
Step 5 becomes —
Be able to state that when a coil and magnet move relatively to one another an e.m.f. is induced in the coil.
And so on.

THE PROGRAMME

Check that you have the following apparatus:
2 similar magnets, their N-poles painted red.
2 coils of wire, one with 40 turns and one with 20 turns.
1 centre reading galvanometer with terminals marked + and — and a needle that moves to the right (towards the + on the scale) when current flows through it from the + terminal to the — terminal.

Connect the two ends of the larger coil to the two terminals of the galvanometer.

Move one magnet, N-pole facing the coil, towards the coil.

Hold it still and then move it away again. Observe the movement of the galvanometer needle.

Work through the following programme, holding a sheet of paper to mask the frames and answers (responses) which follow the one you are dealing with at the moment. Write in the missing words. Check your responses each time you move to the next frame you uncover.

Repeat the experiments when, and as often as you need to do so.

Frame		Response
1.	Whilst the N-pole of the magnet is moving towards the coil, the galvanometer needle is deflected. The needle is deflected by a_____flowing through the galvanometer.	
2.	Whilst the N-pole approaches the coil a _____ flows in the coil circuit.	current
3.	A current also flows in the coil circuit whilst the magnet is _____ away from the coil.	current
4.	When the magnet remains still no_____ flows in the coil.	moving
5.	A current caused by something happening outside the circuit is called an INDUCED current. The current which flows when a magnet moves towards or away from the coil is called an _____ current.	current
6.	Causing an *induced* electric current to flow by making magnetic changes is called electromagnetic _____ ion.	induced
7.	When the magnet moves *towards* the coil the_____ current flows in one direction,	induction
8.	and when it moves away from the coil the_____ flows in the opposite direction.	induced
9.	A current is always driven around a circuit by an e_____ m_____ f_____	induced current
10.	Since the moving magnet gives rise to an induced current it must induce into the coil an_____ to drive this current around the circuit.	electro-motive force (e.m.f.)

161

Frame		Response
11.	When a magnet moves to or from a coil an e.m.f. is_____ in the coil.	e.m.f.
12.	Current can flow only in a complete circuit, but even if the coil is not joined in a circuit an_____ is _____ in it when a magnet moves towards or away from it.	induced
13.	A magnet moving to or from a coil sets up in it an_____ _____	e.m.f. induced
14.	If the coil moved towards or away from the stationary magnet an_____ would flow in the coil.	induced e.m.f.
15.	When both the coil and magnet are still, no_____ is induced in the coil and therefore no _____ _____ flows in the circuit.	induced current Test this by experiment
16.	When the magnet and coil move *relatively* to each other an _____ is induced in the coil.	e.m.f. induced current
17.	Induction effects are caused by the_____ motion of coil and magnet.	e.m.f.
18.	An e.m.f. is induced in a coil by a magnet only so long as they are moving_____to one another.	relative
19.	If the coil and magnet were fixed together and moved together their relative motion would be_____	relative(ly)
20.	in which case no_____ would be_____ in the coil.	zero (nil)
21.	When a double magnetic N-pole moves relatively to the coil, all else being equal the _____ is larger.	e.m.f. induced
22.	When adjacent N & S poles are moved relatively to the coil the_____ _____ is very small (or zero).	induced e.m.f. (or current) Test this by experiment
23.	A strong magnet is associated with more lines of force — a larger magnetic FLUX — than a weak magnet. When a magnet moves relative to a coil the magnetic F_____in the coil changes.	induced e.m.f. (current) Test
24.	When the magnetic_____in a coil changes an e.m.f. is induced in the coil.	flux

Frame		Response
25.	The greater the rate of change of _____ in a coil the greater the induced e.m.f.	flux
26.	No_____ is induced in a coil when the _____ in it is not changing	flux
	Repeat the experiments with the coil of 20 turns in place of the coil with 40 turns.	
27.	For comparable relative movements of the coil and magnet, the e.m.f. _____ in the coil with more turns is _____ than that induced in the coil with fewer turns.	e.m.f. (magnetic) flux
28.	The e.m.f. induced in a coil increases as the rate of change of _____ in it increases	induced greater
29.	and as the number of_____ increases.	flux
30.	The magnitude of the induced e.m.f. increases as the rate of change of _____ x _____ increases.	turns
31.	An e.m.f. is induced in a coil when the number of_____ _____ is changing.	flux-turns
	Now move the magnet and coil relative to each other at varying rates. If they move too quickly the galvanometer will not indicate the current correctly since it will stop flowing before the needle moves.	
32.	When the rate of change of flux-turns is very small the induced e.m.f. is also	flux-turns
33.	As the rate of change of flux-turns increases the_____ _____ increases correspondingly.	small (low)
34.	The magnitude of the e.m.f. induced in a coil by a moving magnet is proportional to (a) the strength of the magnet or the magnetic _____	induced e.m.f. (current)
35.	(b) the _____ ___ _____on the coil	flux
36.	(c) the_____ at which they move relative to one another.	number of turns
37.	This can be summarized — the magnitude of an e.m.f. induced in a circuit is proportional to the _____ of change of _____ x _____ in that circuit.	rate (velocity) (speed)
38.	Write down the full sentence given in frame 37 and then explain it to somebody else.	rate flux-turns

AN INDUCTION COURSE

1. Now that you have successfully completed this experiment work out how you could wind a coil so that however a magnet moves relatively to it there will be virtually no e.m.f. induced in the coil.

   Collect some wire and a short cardboard tube, wind the coil according to your design and then demonstrate and explain your design to the teacher.

   Discuss your design with other students.

2. If the moving magnet causes an (electro-motive) force to act on the conduction electrons, do you think that a still magnet would exert a force on moving electrons?

   Test your view by holding a strong magnet in various positions against the front of a TV set. (The picture is formed by a stream of electrons splashing against the screen.)

3. When a magnet moves relatively to an open circuited coil an e.m.f. is induced in the coil but there is no flow of current around the circuit.

   What then happens to the conduction electrons in the coil whilst the magnet is moving?

Notice the following:

1. The same information is repeated in different ways making increasing demands on the student's understanding but at all times his response is more likely to be right than wrong.

2. The most difficult conceptual step is from frame 8 to frame 9. This leans on the student having successfully acquired a working concept of electromotive force before using this programme. This he should have formed since the concept of e.m.f. is introduced at the beginning of the electricity course and continually reinforced. Notice that in frame 9 the step is almost oversimplified by the prompts e, m and f. This helps to limit the fall in self-confidence which a difficult step would cause.

3. In frames 5 and 23 new words are used — 'induced' and 'flux'. These are given special prominence.

4. The critical statements in the programme are —
   Frame 6 which culminates in the generalizing frame 18.
   Frame 23 which culminates in the generalizing frame 37.

5. Since science is concerned with observation and experiment

and the formulation of empirical laws the principles learned in the programme are not an end in themselves. The student is therefore given problem-solving exercises in which the concepts and principles must be rethought and reorganized. The first two exercises enable him to test the reliability of his thinking whilst the third is designed to promote a deeper insight into the induction process.

Mathematics is, to some extent, programmed by its nature but the logical deductive sequences of the subject are not necessarily the most direct learning sequences. For example, it was found that a programme on the solution of quadratic equations by factorization became more effective when arranged in the following sequence.

1. Any number multiplied by 0 is 0.
2. If $a \times b = 0$ then either a must be 0 or b must be 0.
3. If $(x + 2)(x - 3) = 0$ then either $(x + 2) = 0$ when $x = -2$
   $\qquad\qquad\qquad\qquad$ or $(x - 3) = 0$ when $x = 3$.
4. Given a jumble of terms in x^2, x and numbers (or y^2, y and numbers and so on) they must be arranged to give 2 factors multiplied together = 0.
5. Example.
6. Second example.
7. General statement of procedure.

Here, it became evident that the learners needed to know their objective very clearly before working towards it and they also needed to reinforce their concept of zero.

This, and similar modifications, only come to light when the prototype programme is validated by:
(a) reviewing the responses and
(b) watching and talking to a student as he is using the programme.

SUMMARY

A programme is a coherent body of knowledge broken down into small component steps each designed to produce a small behaviour change and in total causing the student to learn what the programme set out to teach.

In preparing a programme we:
1. Define the desired behavioural objectives.

2. Write the terminal test.
3. Plot the learning sequence.
4. Write the programme.
5. Validate it.

The programme is arranged to:

1. Present teaching in small steps.
2. Require active participation.
3. Give immediate confirmation (or correction).
4. Allow the student to work at his own pace.
5. Make constant revision of the programme possible.

The student for whom the programme is designed should obtain at least 95 per cent correct responses.

Exercise

Preparation of a short programme

OBJECTIVE

To prepare a programme to teach a single item of subject matter, to validate it and analyse the teaching—learning process involved.

The objective is not to produce a conventional professional programme or to know the terms used by programmers but to cause somebody who does not know something to come to know it as a result of an organized written sequence of instruction. Writing the instruction removes the effect of non-verbal communication, of personality, and also the effect of tactical modifications which are made as a consequence of feedback from the learner.

METHOD

1. Pair with a member of the group who has a specialism different from your own. Find one item of subject matter which he does not know, which he would like to know and of which he knows the support material. For example, he might know that there are different kinds of wine but not know the shapes and colours of the bottles in which they are sold or he

might know sufficient background mathematics to learn second order differential equations.

2. Prepare the objective test by which the effectiveness of the programme will be assessed: this is the terminal test.
3. Write the programme in duplicate.
4. Give the programme to the person for whom it has been prepared and observe his reactions very closely, marking difficulties and hesitations on the duplicate copy.
5. Go through the duplicate with him and, by discussion, find out why he experienced difficulties and how they might have been avoided. Find, too, the steps he regarded as redundant ones.
6. Modify the programme to eliminate its defects.

The focal part of the exercise is step 5 since this reveals the strengths and weaknesses of the preparation.

Unit 15

Study Session

Designing self-instructional material

BACKGROUND

The principles which underlie the preparation of material intended to cause learning to happen are little different from the
general principles applicable to learning through group or
tutorial methods. Although these principles have already been
discussed, a kind of shorthand session is useful to the producer
of self-instructional material to act as a series of guidelines for
action and to help him avoid gross errors of presentation.

The following list is a set of useful rules which may be neglected only after testing the programme and finding a special
modification which gives a more direct route to the learning
objective.

1. Very intelligent students or advanced students who are learning subject matter of their own specialism, seem to prefer
   information in the form of abstractions, technical expressions
   and generalizations. They are easily motivated by information
   relevant to their studies because they anticipate success.
   Students of average intelligence are unable to learn new ideas
   unless they are able to see or create visual images to support
   them. Unintelligent students need physical involvement in the
   matter they are learning.
2. We are relatively unable to comprehend details of information
   until we have a vague general idea of the whole of which these
   details are a part.

3. We learn facts and skills by a process of motivation-cue-response-reinforcement.
4. We can attend to only one set of stimuli at a time — any others may act as cues or foci or they may be distractors.
5. Perception can be wayward and we need clear guidance in accurate perception. In general, details should be given in such a way that generalizations are preceded by particular cases, and abstractions are preceded by concrete examples. Essential messages should always dominate the information that supports them.
6. Learners must be able to verbalize important visual information.
7. If the primary objective of the presentation is to cause immediate learning the stimulus-response-reinforcement sequence should be dominant; if it is to motivate the learner the presentation must challenge him and he must anticipate success; if it is designed for attitude orientation the presentation should arouse strong feelings of liking or rejection.

Whatever medium is chosen, every successful presentation will:

Tell the student what he has to learn and/or what he will be able to do at the end of the presentation.

Attract and hold the attention of the student for whom it is prepared.

Remind him of what he already knows in order to learn what is new.

Give cues which lead him to predict what he is about to learn.
Give feedback to tell him when he is successful.

Provide conditions likely to promote the kind of retention required.

Imply or provide a means of enabling the student to assess his own performance.

PREPARATION OF DESIGNS

There follows now a description of the way in which material designed to enable students to learn on their own — mediated learning material — may be prepared. To give a measure of realism, four examples are chosen, each with special communication characteristics — loop film, video-tape, slide-tape, and tape-text. The reader should become familiar with the characteristics of each and then prepare a package for mediated learning choosing his mode to suit the students for whom it is intended and the subject matter to be taught.

The objective of this and the next unit is threefold:

1. To focus the reader's attention on a short specific teaching—learning exercise in which no tactical modification will be possible. In other words, he will not be able to put his mistakes right by changing the sequence or style, or by the pressure of his personality whilst the learning is taking place as is possible in a live lesson. In this way he can test the effectiveness of his teaching strategies.

2. To provide the reader with first-hand experience of the problems of selecting appropriate modes of mediated learning presentations.

3. To enable him, by testing the effectiveness of his material, to make modifications to it and, in the light of successive assessments, find for himself the most effective ways of teaching.

The four types of learning material which have been chosen have, in very general terms, the following characters:

Film — almost exclusively visual communication.
Video-tape — visual communication with verbal support.
Slide-tape — verbal communication with visual support.
Tape-text — almost exclusively verbal.

Each of these modes of communication offers special teaching opportunities which can be exploited and each has weaknesses which should be understood and, if possible compensated for. Every teacher who is likely to exploit media — and this means almost every teacher — should at least be acquainted with the strengths and weaknesses of different forms of mediated learning. This is probably best learned through the preparation and testing of media materials in some form or another.

LOOP FILMS OR SHORT FILMS

Loop films are lengths of 8 mm film with their ends joined together so that once they are in a loop film projector, they run from beginning to end over and over again until the instrument is switched off (Fig. 24). The film is sealed in a plastic cassette and may be of any length from about 2 metres (half a minute running time) to 15 metres (4 minutes running time). They are silent films. Short 15 metre non-loop films may also be shown in suitable projectors and then rewound for reviewing in much the same way as tape is rewound in a tape recorder.

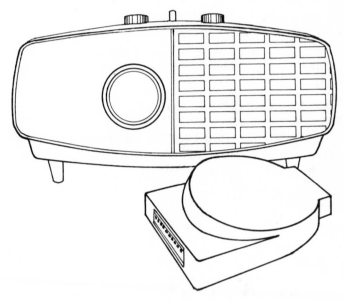

Fig. 24 A loop-film projector and cassette

The four special characteristics of silent loop (or short) films which can be exploited are:
1. The information is communicated entirely visually.
2. A film can show movement.
3. A loop film (or a short non-loop film) can be viewed over and over again and consequently offers repetition.
4. It is brief.
Such a film is therefore appropriate for the communication of certain concepts which the learner needs to reflect on as he is being prompted visually. Examples of such concepts include those of magnetic field, crop rotation, servo-control and colour harmony.

In preparing a concept film, it is important to think of the context in which it will be used. For instance, a film on magnetic fields would be ONE of the contributions to a learner's understanding. He would probably carry out his own experiments, read about magnetic fields and so on and the film should therefore be designed primarily to make its own unique contribution to his understanding. It might follow the pattern:

(*a*) The earth with its N and S poles.

(*b*) A magnet swinging freely and coming to rest with the end pointing N becoming labelled 'North Seeking Pole' and then becoming red in colour (the colour generally used to denote the N pole).

(*c*) The magnet changing into a compass needle with its N end coloured red.

(*d*) A stationary magnet with compass needles moving towards it one at a time to become lines of magnetic force.

And so on.

(*a*)　　　　(*b*)　　　　(*c*)　　　　(*d*)　　　　(*e*)

In this way the changing visual scene cues the learner's thinking until he begins to be able to 'see' in his mind the magnetic character of the space around a magnet as clearly as he is able to see concrete objects.

When he carries out experiments a student's curiosity or his teacher, cause him to move things and look at things in order to learn and often the objective in the learner's mind is to predict what will happen next rather than to build up a meaningful mental construction of why it happens. This *doing* phase however, constitutes a sound base level of learning. Discussion and thinking refines the effect of the doing and the loop film might well offer the final stage of organizing these refined ideas into the coherent beginnings of a fully structured concept (Gagné: see ref. on p. 83).

Short films are also particularly suitable for the demonstration of certain skills — of tying knots, starting techniques in running a race, the preparing and giving of injections, and so on. In such cases, the learner must do more than see the film. He must practice, probably be told things by an instructor, probably watch experts. But the film can give him the sequenced visual information which, once he has become accustomed to it, will enable him to acquire the skill more quickly and more expertly.

One special advantage of the film is that it can show what a movement looks like to the skilled performer himself — for this the camera is held alongside the performer's face: it has a privileged viewpoint. This has particular value in skills such as tying knots where the right-hand, left-hand relationships are of major consequence (Fig. 25).

In general, skill films will show the skill performed a number of times at the correct speed in order to communicate the general rhythmical pattern of the whole, it will then select critical or difficult components for emphasis — superimposed pointers, slow-motion, captions, animations or close-up shots — and put them together so that they become the whole skill performed at the correct speed again. In these films, animations

Fig. 25 The privileged viewpoint

and visual cues such as rings and arrows appearing over important components are usually more valuable than live photography.

For association learning the film can show items which the learner must connect together, presented in such a way as to cue the connection in the learner's mind. For example, a picture of a plant can be followed by a brief shot of its name and then its habitat, or an increasing voltage can be linked with an increasing current. In these kinds of circumstances particularly, although by no means exclusively, the sequence should be designed to invoke verbal anticipatory responses in the viewer. (Galparin.) For example, he might, as he looks, say to himself 'The voltage increases . . . so the current increases', and if the visual sequence is designed to fit in with this statement so that he sees the voltage increase, says to himself that the current increases and then immediately afterwards sees it increase, the operant conditioning effect will enhance the learning (Skinner). This process can be triggered by using pointers, close-ups or captions. Of course, loop films are also valuable for simply showing what something looks like — a sculpture or a crystal structure — but this objective is too easily achieved to constitute a useful exercise at this stage.

Making a loop film or a short film for repeated viewing

The decision to make a loop film will stem from a number of teaching needs and from a careful assessment of the merits of this mode of presentation compared with alternatives. In general the following are reasons for making a film:

1. To provide a brief coherent sequence of visual information for as many times as the learner requires.
2. To show visuals in which movement enhances understanding or where movement is an essential component.
3. To show visuals from a 'privileged' viewpoint.
4. To provide an 'all round' view of something.
5. To slow down or speed up a movement.

There are, of course, others.

OBJECTIVES AND TEST

The first step is to write down the objective of the film and the ability of the learner for whom it is intended. For example:

To teach first year nautical students, unaided, how to make a reef knot.

To teach A-level students the generation of a sine wave on a CRO so that they will be able to set up and operate the equipment in the laboratory.

To provide members of an adult evening class with an interesting basis for French conversation; to motivate them.

At the same time a test is prepared to indicate the level of attainment that will be reached if the film is successful.

Secondly, it is useful to predict the kind of learning the film is intended to evoke — principle learning, concept structuring, ego-involvement, associationism or conditioning.

Next, a story board should be prepared. To do this, write each element of the action on cards and pin these, in sequence, to a board (Fig. 26). Since this will give an immediate impression of the film as a whole it can be refined and re-organized prior to scripting. The abbreviations needed for scripting are as follows:

Pan — to rotate camera in a horizontal arc. This should be carried out very slowly and steadily.

Tilt — to tilt the camera up or down.

Track in/out — to move the camera towards/away from the object.

Zoom in/out — to operate the zoom control to make the object appear nearer/more distant.

Cut — to change instantly from one shot to another.

Long shot (LS) — main object forms a small part of the main scene.

Medium long shot (MLS) — Group is dominant in its surroundings.

Medium shot (MS) — object is dominant in its surroundings.

Close-up shot (CS) — object fills the screen.

Big close-up shot (BCU) — part of object fills screen.

Normal angle shot (NA) — camera pointing horizontally.

Fig. 26 A story board

High angle shot (HA) — camera above and slanting down.
Low angle shot (LA) — camera below and slanting upwards.
The most critical rules to observe when writing a script are:
1. Minimum shot length 2 seconds.
2. Change shot every 2—11 seconds unless the subject matter
   demands sustained attention from a single viewpoint.
3. When changing the shot distance always change the camera
   position as well.
4. When filming a moving subject never take two adjacent shots
   from opposite directions: an intermediate shot 'takes' viewers
   to the new viewpoint.
5. When changing shots of a movement never begin the second
   shot by repeating the end of the first one.

It is advisable to arrange the script in columns (see p. 00). The
first column gives the shot number so that each shot can be identi-
fied. It is a wise precaution to cross off each shot as it is taken so
that no sequencing mistakes occur. The second column gives the
time of each separate shot and the third shows the cumulative time.
The fourth column describes the shots, the fifth one the action and
a sixth column can be used for any special notes. The shots in
column four can be drawn or described. The final entry in the
third column should be 200 seconds or less. When using standard-
8 film there must be a break in the script after 100 seconds or
less to allow for the film to be turned over in the camera.

Having prepared the script its film potential should be estima-
ted by a trial run with the camera unloaded. Each shot should be
timed by an observer with a stop watch who reports on whether
it seems to be the right length for a viewer. Camera positions
and actions as well as shot timings may be changed at this stage
in order to make the film 'seem' right to the producer.

Captions may be written or drawn in colour on a chalkboard,
built up on a felt board or specially prepared on matt card with
sides in the ratio of 4 to 3.

If a choice of location is possible it is easiest to film most
things in daylight out of doors rather than in artificial light in-
doors. And it is always wisest to use a very robust tripod and
cable release if this is possible.

For indoor filming the lighting must be adjusted to give the best kind of shadow effects and to show up or eliminate the background, depending on the subject. Good lighting is essential.

Unpredictable shots — of animals or birds for example — involve setting the camera with the distance 'about right' and shooting only if the subject appears within the focal area. The camera should be held in the hand for a quick manoeuvre, and the subject can be followed in one direction but, in general, not to and fro.

Fig. 27 A film crew

When the film has been processed it should be viewed once or twice by projecting it in a super-8 projector so that a note can be made of any bad or unwanted material. These sections are located with an editor and then removed. The film is then spliced and finally sent to be cassetted.

If technical or planning mistakes are made the film will need cutting and joining together again and whilst this presents no problems, the joins are sometimes noticeable during projection and, of course, they may break if they are badly made. A shooting script is drawn up as follows.

SHOT	T_1	T_2	SHOT	ACTION	NOTES
1	4	4	(1kg) NACS	A sphere marked 1 kg in space brightly lit against a black starry background.	Use expanded polystyrene sphere for kilogramme. Dark blue background with pin-holes – rear lighting.
2	4	8	1kg O NALS	Animate.	Move kg to reduce its size but keep background size constant.
3	2	10	1kg 1N ⬇ O	Animate. Mass with arrow accelerates across $\frac{1}{8}$" width of frame – camera still. 1N initially over arrow.	
4	4	14	1kg ⬅O 1N 1m/s²	Animate. Mass with arrow moves off frame.	Cut as kg moves off frame.

SHOT	T_1	T_2	SHOT	ACTION	NOTES
5	4	18	1kg ⃝	Mass of 1 kg in space	Camera turned to produce angled motion and shots 2–4 repeated.
6	2	20	1kg	Animate. Mass with arrow accelerates in direction of arrow.	
7	4	24	1kg ⃝ 1m/s²	Animate. Mass moves off frame leaving captions behind.	Cut as kg moves off frame.
8	4		2kg N/kg	None.	2 kg about $1\frac{1}{4}$ × diameter of 1 kg.

SHOT	T_1	T_2	SHOT	ACTION	NOTES
9	4	32	2kg NALS	2 kg with arrow accelerates at half previous rate.	Camera and background turned with mass moving horizontally.
10	8	40	2kg 1N 0.5m/s²	Mass moves off frame.	
11	4	44	NACS 1kg	None.	
12	2	46	1kg NALS 2N	Mass accelerates.	

SHOT	T_1	T_2	SHOT	ACTION	NOTES
13	2	48		Mass accelerates.	Continue shooting.
	3	51		None.	
14	4	55		Mass hanging on support.	
15	5	60		String cut with scissors and mass falls. Caption and arrow remain.	

182

SHOT	T_1	T_2	SHOT	ACTION	NOTES
16	4	64	1kg 9·81m/s² →	Mass on string.	
17	5	69	9·81m/s² → 9·81N	Caption added.	
18	3	72	2kg	Mass on string.	
19	5	77	↓9·81m/s² 2kg	String out. Captions remain.	

183

SHOT	T_1	T_2	SHOT	ACTION	NOTES
20	4	84	2kg 9·81m/s² → (Mass on string diagram)	Mass on string.	
21	5	86	2kg 9·81m/s² → 19·62N (diagram)	Caption added.	
22	5	91	Force = mass x acceleration.	None.	

VIDEO-TAPED LESSON

Video tapes have many characteristics in common with silent films but they offer sound in addition. This enables the producer to assist the learner with the verbalization of the information. At the same time, it opens up the danger of relieving the learner of making efforts after understanding and of creating his own verbal construction. If he makes no effort the learner will be lulled into a sense of security; of believing he knows simply because the information fits together so obviously. Consequently, the producer of video taped lessons should keep in mind two additional principles:

1. We can *attend* to only one source of information at a time: either the sound will be dominant or the vision will be dominant. Generally the producer should deliberately arrange for one to be in the foreground and the other in the background.
2. Learning is generally enhanced if the learner verbally antici- pates what he is going to see and then afterwards receives verbal reinforcement of his response.

MAKING A VIDEO-TAPED LESSON

The initial preparation of the script follows the same pattern as that for loop films. The abbreviations used in scripting include those given for cine together with:

Fade-up (FU) — picture gradually appears.
Fade-out (FO) — picture gradually disappears.
Animate — start moving cartoon or model.
Superimpose (SI) — two pictures from two cameras shown simultaneously.

The script describes both the vision and the sound, with vision on the left-hand side and sound on the right. The timing is mainly controlled by the commentary. Perhaps the most impor- tant differences between making a film and a video-tape are:

1. The video-tape can be played back immediately and, if neces- sary, remade without waste of film or time.
2. Once shooting begins the entire sequence must be taped with- out a break and no corrections can be made as the shooting continues.

Example of video tape script MEASURING ATMOSPHERIC PRESSURE

SHOT No.	CAMERA No. & TYPE OF SHOT	VISION	SOUND
1	2	Collapsing oil drum	
2	S/I 1	Caption 'Measuring Atmospheric Pressure'	
3	F/O 1	M.S. Presenter	In the last lesson we discovered that the pressure of the atmosphere was great enough to crush an iron oil drum and, after the TV lesson you did some experiments to find out more about this pressure. Here is one of the experiments you did.
	Cut to 1		
4	Cut to 2	C.U. Tumber	I wonder if you spilled the water. You filled the tumbler to the brim, and then carefully pushed the card across the top taking great care not to leave any air between the card and the water. You then turned the tumbler upside down and, if you were successful, . . . the water remained inside.
5	Cut to 1	M.S. Presenter	I am sure you realized that the card was held in place by . . . the pressure of the air.
6	Cut to 2	10 sec. Cap. 'Air pressure'	Now, the water in this tumbler weighs about 300 grams
		Animate	and the area covered by the card is about 30 square centimetres. So what do we know about the pressure of the atmosphere? . . . Yes, it must be at least
		End animation	
7	Cut to 1	M.S. Presenter	. . . 10 grammes per square centimetre which is at least a thousand newtons per square metre, to use the correct units.

8	C.U. Cap 2	(Slowly) C.U. Cape 2	Well, today we are going to be more precise and *calculate* the pressure of the atmosphere by finding the force it exerts on a known area. And to do this I am going to use a pump. Here is a pump which is used for pumping up the tyres of motor cars — with two differences . . . 1. I have plugged the outlet hole and . . . 2. I have turned the pump piston upside down so that it is like a parachute.
1		(Slowly) M.S. Presenter	Just to make absolutely sure that there is no air above the piston I have put some vaseline into the pump barrel .
10	2	L.S. Presenter to Apparatus Stand	Now watch. When I pull the piston out and let go of it . . . it is pushed back again by? . . . that's right . . . by the pressure of the atmosphere. Our job now is to find the *force* needed to pull the piston out of the pump barrel, the *area* of the piston and then to divide the force by the area. Here is your first problem. Why don't I subtract the area of the piston rod from the area of the piston when I calculate the pressure? Now let me show you what I should like *you* to do for yourselves.
1	1	Tilt down and zoom to weights. L.S. Presenter	First of all, support your pump in a suitable stand. Make sure that the piston is pushed to the top of the cylinder and then load it with weights until you discover the force which just pulls the piston free. From this and the area you should be able to find the atmospheric pressure.
			Once again . . . support the pump . . . push in the piston to exclude all the air . . . load and finally calculate. Next week we can talk about the answers you get and then say something about the effects of air pressure in everyday life.
		F/O Sound and vision	

SLIDE-TAPE LESSON

This consists of a series of slides, some of which may be blank and some may contain verbal information, together with a sound tape. The slide projection is controlled by impulses on the tape as it passes through a synchronizer. This may be an integral part of the tape recorder or separate from it. Synchronizing the tape requires no technical skill when up-to-date equipment is used (Fig. 28).

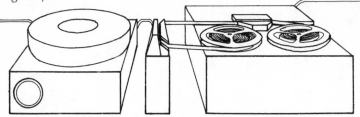

Fig. 28 A tape-slide synchronizing equipment

With this mode of presentation, the continuity and the motivation to learn rather than to simply look, is generally dominated by the sound track. The illustration, which should of course be critical to the comprehensibility of the message acts as a focal area of interest as well as an information source. The method is likely to be the most useful wherever explanations need static visual references such as would occur for example, in a lesson on the evolution of a mammal, or the architecture of a town. In preparing this type of presentation the initial stage will again include writing the objective, defining the target student and predicting the kind of learning that the presentation will evoke.

The verbal script is generally thought about first and then the slides prepared and sequenced. The final script is then written to match the slides.

Because of its dominant role in directing the learner, the commentary should be designed to invite responses by putting critical words at the ends of sentences, by pauses, rhetorical questions and repetitions. Since the learner can attend to only one thing at a time, words and pictures should either give the same message or one should be given priority.

Here is part of the script of a tape-slide lesson. There are two ways of synchronizing the two: one is to record the script and operate the slide projector through the synchronizer at the same time; the other to record the speech first and then dub the synchronizing pulses during playback. The latter method has advantages in certain cases.

SLIDE No.	COMMENTARY	ILLUSTRATION
		(This would normally be written)
7	Just outside the walls of the Castle is the Cathedral (1 sec) This too is Norman (2 sec)	
8	Its West Front looks towards the River Medway and	
9	the great West Doorway is one of the most perfect examples of late Norman work — its beautifully recessed arch is filled with rich carving (10 sec)	
10	The nave — the oldest cathedral nave in England is sheer delight — pure Norman (6 sec)	

The script for a tape-slide lesson is simpler in appearance than that for a film or video-tape but the word sequence and timing demand a constant critical awareness of the mental processes they should evoke and preparation is therefore more rather than less important.

TAPE-TEXT LESSON

This is often found to be the most successful of the various kinds of mediated learning modes: it is also one of the least expensive. It consists of a tape recording and a written text — usually in duplicated form so that it can be used by the student for written work during the learning session and then kept as a record. The written and sound texts may together constitute a programme in the conventional sense but this is justifiable only if a written text on its own provides insufficient motivation.

The most basic use for such a combination is in teaching about subjects in which sound is critical — about music, poetry, public speaking, the physics of sound and so on, but in all other cases the tape recording is most likely to be exclusively spoken words and almost always the dominant prime motivator. Since the written material generally calls either for study or the completion of exercises, the learner is instructed to switch off the tape recorder before starting to read or write, thus:
'. . . and grain crops are grown in the lower lying areas to the east. In a few moments I want you to switch off and then, referring to the same map, answer the questions on the top of page 3. When you have done so, switch on again. Now switch off'.

Naturally, this type of presentation can follow the conventional type of programmed text arrangement very closely and the student's progress can be monitored with precision.

Exercise

Discuss the structure and form of the loop film given on pages 179 to 184 and then the video-tape programme on pages 186 to 187 and predict the kind of learning processes to which they give rise. Discuss the choice of media for these two lessons and argue the advantages and disadvantages of alternatives.

Discuss the teaching scheme within which these lessons might fit and the manner in which their values could be assessed.

Study Session

A systematic approach to learning

OBJECTIVES

There is more to teaching than teaching well. Satan is probably
as capable a teacher as can be found in any technical college and
yet he misses out on his objectives. He would undoubtedly get a
distinction in his teachers' certificate and his arguments for
pragmatism would single him out as a student of outstanding
honesty — truthful enough to justify the philosophy by which
he operates. But his objective is to have us all in hell and this is
not nice.

So in choosing objectives we would do well to decide what
our long-term aims are. In coming to this decision we might do
worse than find a man who does well what we want to teach
and then find out what it is that makes him good at it. It is
often a shock to discover how little this man can do of what we
thought the syllabus should include. It is sometimes more of a
shock to discover what we want to include in the syllabus
because we ourselves know about it, or because it enhances our
mystique or because it helps to fill out the days. But we should
be ruthless in our choice of objectives and base it on real men
living real lives and performing real jobs.

We begin, then, by analysing the behaviour of the man who
has successfully learned what we intend to teach. In doing so we
should decide what kind of knowing and what level of knowing
enables him to operate successfully. We should sift what he
thinks from what he feels and what he does — the cognitive,
affective and psychomotor aspects. Then we should try to discover what learning has resulted from conditioning, from rote
learning, from the exercise of short-term memory, from concept

structuring, from practising perceptual motor skills, from engaging in problem solving activities and so on. We should try to discover, too, what has been learned unwittingly and what requires external motivation, critical planning and organizing. And this is asking for the near impossible. So we do our best.

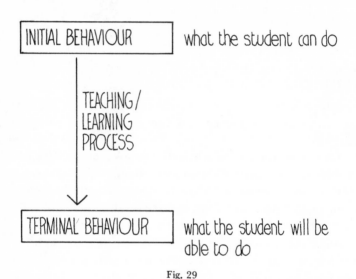

INITIAL BEHAVIOUR — what the student can do

TEACHING / LEARNING PROCESS

TERMINAL BEHAVIOUR — what the student will be able to do

Fig. 29

Such a task analysis throws up a list of abilities that the successful student will have at the end of the course. The next step is to decide which of these the student should already have acquired since these need not be included in the syllabus. Thus, for example, a Concorde conversion course for pilots of jet aircraft would be suitable only for people who were already familiar with the concepts, facts and skills needed to fly jet aircraft and equally, a lesson on the addition of vulgar fractions would be appropriate only for students able to add and multiply integers.

The beginner student who already has the competencies chosen by the course planner is often called the target student — the student at whom the learning can be directed effectively. If, now the target student's abilities are removed from those revealed in the task analysis, the remaining list is the syllabus (Fig. 29).

The syllabus is now structured to form a course by converting it to a scheme of work and this will throw up stages of development each with its own objective. Once these are known, the learning strategies and the learning media can be decided upon — for example, an objective might probably best be reached by the use of a film followed by discussion, or another by a series of graded exercises with tutorial assistance and objective testing and so on.

At the same time as the terminal abilities are chosen, the terminal test should be prepared. This must be tested, or validated, so that those who have acquired the desired competency will pass it and those who fall short in any particular aspect, do not.

It is useful to set the test to, say 50 people, 25 of whom are clearly novices and 25 are fully trained. The marks will reflect these differences if the test is reliable.

With the scheme, strategies, media and test in being, the teaching-learning sequence can now be followed to completion. The learners should be set the final test (or one like it) at the start of the course so that any students who are already able to pass it can be moved to the next stage in the programme. This test is called the pre-test. At the end of the course, the learners are tested again and the test scrutinized and, if necessary, modified in the light of their performance. Finally, the course is evaluated and the procedure repeated in the light of its effectiveness. This cyclic development, with single factors varied on an experimental basis leads to changes which the course manager regards as desirable: greater cost-effectiveness, increased opportunities for study in other fields: changed deployment of scarce staff and so on (Fig. 30).

In practice, we cannot always make ideal provision of this kind: it is not always possible to provide precisely the kind of materials that are needed nor is the space always available for certain of the learning activities. Consequently there needs to be a control analysis or front-end analysis which makes quite clear the constraints within which the curriculum designer must work. Although this seems so fundamental that it should be made earlier in time than the ideal design, it is useful to plan the ideal

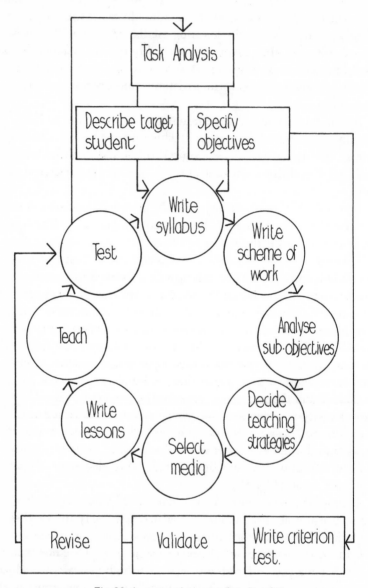

Fig. 30 A systematic approach to learning

first since this gives a clearly defined goal to work for and makes estimating for the future more precise. It is therefore more progressive to produce the ideal curriculum and then modify it to accommodate the constraints, than to accept inadequate conditions as the base for planning. The constraints that must be accepted are:

    number of students in the group;
    classroom and workplace available;
    times and dates of course;
    equipment and money available,

and so on: indeed any circumstance which interferes with the pattern of study derived from the theoretical plan. These should be retained on the planning board as negative factors which forward planning and estimating should try to eliminate.

RESOURCES AND LIBRARIES

A systematic approach to learning, such as has been outlined, presupposes that a range of facilities and materials exist and that they can be found and used as and when they are needed. This latter requirement is met, in the case of books, by the conventional college library staffed by a trained librarian staff. However, materials and equipment other than books are involved in certain teaching-learning circumstances and these have become sufficiently numerous and varied for the whole question of resources for learning to call for special study in the context of the overall planning of the college and the deployment of its staff.

THE OBJECTIVE

The objective of providing colleges as places in which students learn is rarely examined and yet there is no supernatural edict that requires societies to gather young people in herds and educate them together. Indeed, it has not always happened and does not even now happen in every culture.

However, having argued a case for colleges, three reasons for having them stand out:

    to provide a highly charged learning environment;

to reinforce and enhance motivation;

to provide learning resources.

Now, when learning resources consisted of little more than a few books, a chalkboard and chalk, the college was built around the performance of the teacher: in other words, colleges were teacher centred institutions. But now there are many resources, some are useful in teacher-directed learning, some for student self learning and some for both. Between them, teacher and resources make it possible for students to learn:

(a) alone — assignments, private study, correspondence course, Open University course;

(b) in small groups — tutorials, seminars, lessons;

(c) in large groups — lectures, team teaching, theatre, and to learn best in equally varied places.

The spectrum of teaching-learning circumstances can therefore be seen as one that stretches from teacher assisted learning at the one end to resources assisted learning at the other, thus:

Teacher-assisted learning	Teacher/resource learning	Resource-assisted learning
Lessons, lectures, tutorials, seminars, live demonstration, discussion.	Team teaching, projects, assignments, discovery learning.	All forms of private study and research.

The learning opportunities opened up by this provision must now be matched by the physical environmental provision and by staff competencies. A college might therefore be designed for its dual function with:

(a) teacher-assisted learning spaces

classrooms, lecture theatres, seminar rooms, tutorial rooms, discussion spaces, practical rooms, common rooms.

(b) resource assisted learning spaces

book library, film, tape, disc, transparency, etc. library, reading rooms, viewing and listening spaces, equipment library containing apparatus such as tape recorders and record players (Fig. 31).

The provision is also reflected in the staffing which might take the form shown on p. 198.

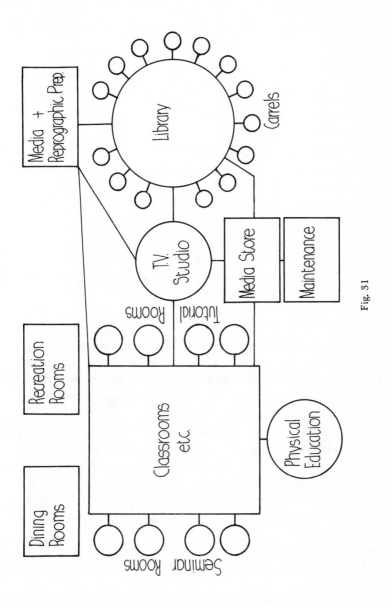

Fig. 31

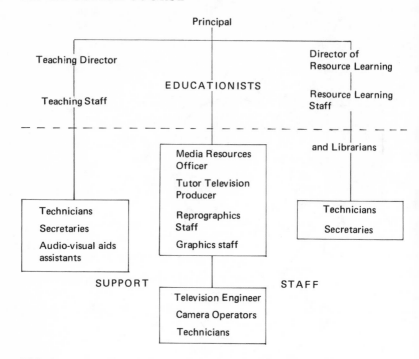

This in turn calls for a reappraisal of staff competencies. In particular the Director of Resource Learning would probably need to be an educational psychologist with experience in the storage and retrieval of data and with some management experience. He might therefore be a librarian with qualifications in psychology and resource learning or a teacher with special qualifications in psychology and experience in resource management and librarianship. This pattern of staffing tends to involve many non-teachers in the teaching-learning arena and should, we hope, throw up teachers as the professionals they should be with a proper and competent support staff just as surgeons are supported by nursing staff, radiographers, radiologist, pathologist and so on. The old type of teacher whose competencies ranged from serving meals to playing the piano with a real concern for registration and an aversion from adult observers in his classroom has become obsolete.

The staff organization will more and more reflect the importance of the professional qualities we expect of teachers rather

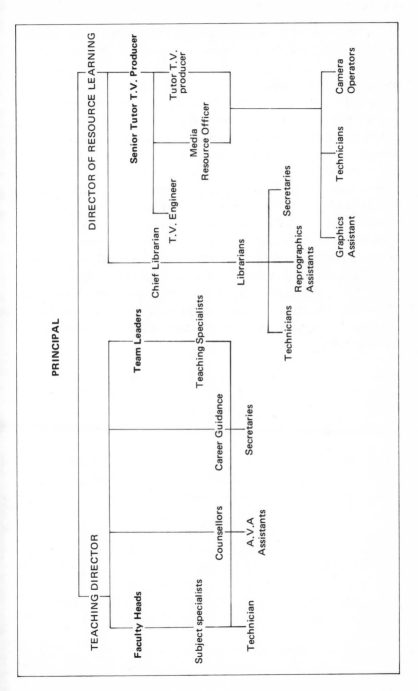

PRINCIPAL

TEACHING DIRECTOR

DIRECTOR OF RESOURCE LEARNING

Faculty Heads

Subject specialists

Technician

Counsellors

A.V.A Assistants

Career Guidance

Secretaries

Team Leaders

Teaching Specialists

Chief Librarian

T.V. Engineer

Senior Tutor T.V. Producer

Tutor T.V. producer

Media Resource Officer

Technicians

Librarians

Reprographics Assistants

Secretaries

Graphics Assistant

Technicians

Camera Operators

than their managerial abilities, and promotion prospects will be opened for the teacher who wants to remain involved at the work face of the college. Such a structure might be the one shown on the previous page.

Here the dedicated teacher could progress through team leader to be a teaching director and still be closely involved in teaching. Equally, the dedicated subject specialist could follow a similarly progressive promotional career. But more than this, there should be career opportunities for everyone on the staff. Technicians and secretaries, graphics assistants and camera men who have the interest and ability should be given the opportunity to study, qualify and progress along whatever route is appropriate to their competencies so that no member of the team feels the deadweight of having started a blind alley career.

In these circumstances, the systematic planning of learning could take place in a fertile environment; one in which both the material and human resources would be properly deployed and organized to implement the findings of educational research and investigation.

Unit 16

Exercise

Preparation of a learning package

OBJECTIVE

To prepare a set of self-instructional material for the learning of a single new item — preferably a new concept or alternatively a new skill.

The overall objective is to provide a highly concentrated exercise in methodology where the success or failure of the teaching is independent of modifications or afterthoughts introduced by the teacher whilst the learner is learning. It calls for a degree of precision and pedagogical insight above that demanded by face to face teaching where human qualities of sympathy, humour, enthusiasm and so on can, and do, more than offset poor planning and a lack of understanding of psychological and educational principles. Furthermore, it affords an opportunity of testing and modifying the material so that more information about learning can be gleaned after the completion of this course.

It must be stressed that the exercise is an exercise in method and not in technical manipulation or artistic production. Indeed, there seems to be little or no correlation between the expertness with which material is drawn and constructed and the success of that material as a source of learning.

Nevertheless, there will be an unwitting effect — an influence of quality, standards, design and skill — on the learner, which may have nothing to do with the central learning objective of the material but which undoubtedly finds a place in all overall educational objectives. Consequently, the methodological quality of the work is of dominant importance: the production matters.

It must also be stressed that the preparation of learning material is an arduous, professional occupation. Writing a short programme, validating it and so on requires training and experience (some would hold that it requires a long course and a City and Guilds qualification) and consequently at this stage it is wise to choose the amount of subject matter to be taught with a measure of modesty. But equally, provided the task is faced as an exercise in method it can be an invaluable experience for the new teacher.

PROCEDURE

1. Write down, in behavioural terms, the objective of the learning material.
2. Prepare a test — objective if possible — to designate the level of learned behaviour of the student.
3. Describe the student for whom the material is intended and, if relevant, prepare a test to reject those without the pre-knowledge and skills needed to commence the learning.
4. Write down the kind of learning sequences and processes that will most likely lead to efficient learning.
5. Write down the kind of communication process that should dominate the teaching and then write down the support modes.
6. Select the media to provide these communicate links.
7. Prepare cards and a story board (as for making a loop film) using different coloured cards for the different media in the package.
8. Write down the programme.
9. Make a dummy run and discuss and modify it.
10. Produce the material.
11. Test it.

Every member of the course should complete the exercise if time permits. If not, every member should complete the first seven steps.

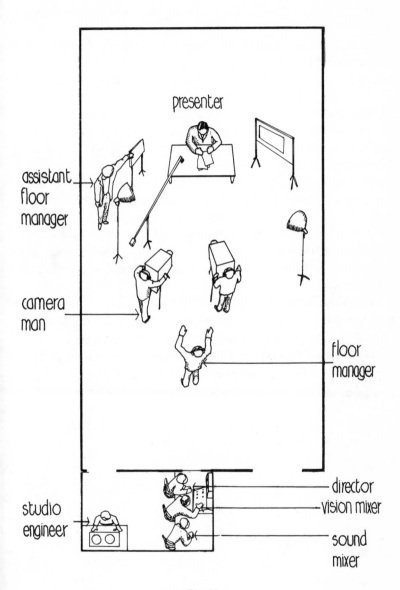

Fig. 32

Steps 9 and 10 generally involve group work and if film or video-tape are involved group work is essential. Groups of four or five working together are able to expedite production and also reduce preparation inadequacies. For filming, the division of responsibilities might be:

A. Producer (the member whose material is being produced. He takes overall control).

B. Cameraman.

C. Stop-watch man (who counts down and times the shots)

D. and possibly E are available for the many jobs that invariably arise.

For television work, if there are two cameras, there will be two cameramen, one presenter and one floor manager, together with the producer who will operate the vision mixer controls: there may be others. Fig. 32 shows a full team. This means a minimum of five people to a group. With only one camera, the group size can be reduced to three or even, under some circumstances, two.

However, above all else, remember that this is an exercise in method: the objective is to know more about teaching and not to qualify as an artist or technician. Furthermore, this is a closely focused exercise in pedagogical precision which, in the end, sorts out the professionals from the pop stars.

Index

INDEX

INDEX